CONTINUITY, CHANCE AND CHANGE

CONTINUITY, CHANCE AND CHANGE

The character of the industrial revolution in England

E. A. WRIGLEY

*Professor of Population Studies, London School of
Economics and Political Science*

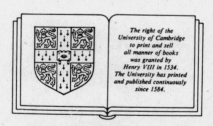

The right of the
University of Cambridge
to print and sell
all manner of books
was granted by
Henry VIII in 1534.
The University has printed
and published continuously
since 1584.

Cambridge University Press
Cambridge
New York   New Rochelle   Melbourne   Sydney

Published by the Press Syndicate of the University of Cambridge
The Pitt Building, Trumpington Street, Cambridge CB2 1RP
32 East 57th Street, New York, NY 10022, USA
10 Stamford Road, Oakleigh, Melbourne 3166, Australia

First published 1988

Printed in Great Britain at Cambridge University Press

British Library cataloguing in publication data

Wrigley, E.A. (Edward Anthony)
Continuity, chance and change: the character of the industrial revolution in
England.
1. England. Industrialisation, 1700–1900.
I. Title 338'. 0942

Library of Congress cataloguing in publication data

Wrigley, E.A. (Edward Anthony), 1931–Continuity, chance and change.
Bibliography.
Includes index.
1. England–Industries–History–19th century.
2. England–Economic conditions–19th century.
3. England–Social conditions–19th century. I. Title. HC255.W83
1988 338.0942 88–1032

ISBN 0 521 35648 2

AL

To the memory of my father

Contents

Figures and tables

Introduction

This book began as the Ellen McArthur lectures delivered in the University of Cambridge in the Lent Term 1987. The invitation extended to me by the Managers of the Fund to deliver the lectures was both an honour that I deeply appreciated, and an opportunity that was most welcome in that I had been turning over in my mind for some time a topic that seemed appropriate for the lectures. Receiving the invitation also obliged me to make a decision over which I might otherwise have deliberated much longer. After many years spent in work principally concerned with the population history of England, I had returned increasingly to my first main research interest, the better understanding of the industrial revolution. I was keen to look again both at some very general issues of interpretation and at a number of substantive matters where there seemed hope of progress. My dilemma lay in deciding between a large-scale general book on the industrial revolution to be written only after carrying out the substantive work and a short, programmatic review. The former could not have been written for several years; the latter, since it could be written in advance of carrying out most of the empirical work, could be embarked on forthwith. The Managers' invitation decided me in favour of the latter.

There was a further decision to be made when the lectures had been delivered. Some earlier Ellen McArthur lectures were published with little change from the form in which they were delivered; others have been much extended and re-written before publication. I was predisposed to make as little change as possible to the original text, given the circumstances in which the lectures came to be written. In

1

the event, the present text differs rather more from the original than I had initiallly envisaged. First, it seemed useful at several points in the text to include figures or tables. In some cases the development of the argument was modified by the inclusion of the new material. Second, the constraints of a set of public lectures, each intended to be delivered in fifty-five to sixty minutes, are arbitrary, imposing a close similarity of length between the lectures and making it difficult to avoid compressing some passages excessively. Converted to a written form the lectures were freed from these constraints, and some sections are rather longer in consequence. Third, public lectures have no footnotes as delivered. Most of the footnotes that have now been incorporated into the text were written after the lectures were given. Where the footnotes dealt with substantive questions, rather than simply providing authority for quotations and assertions in the main body of the text, their writing sometimes meant changing the main text.

For all these reasons the present text and the original text differ somewhat. There has, however, been no change to the scope or thrust of the argument. The four chapters of the present book were the four lectures and the sequence of the argument in each of them retains its original form. Nor have I modified the literary style of the lectures, other than marginally. The style betrays the origin of the work as the spoken rather than the written word. It remains assertive, and perhaps occasionally controversial in tone; programmatic rather than monographic; as much intended to provoke as to persuade.

By an astounding irony of modern historiography, the industrial revolution, whose intrinsic interest and importance should make it the most exciting topic of study among all the 'big' issues of the history of the development of the modern world, has become a dull subject that slips into focus and out again, uncomfortably peripheral to the vision of many historians. The stage is peopled with other characters. Hamlet is often performed without the Prince of Denmark.

There are good reasons why this should be so. No one can be in doubt about the extent of the difference between the pre-industrial world and the world today. The industrial revolution is a convenient label to attach to that part of the transformation which is principally economic in nature. But labelling falls well short of coherent description, much less convincing explanation, and in their absence interest in the phenomenon has languished. The term industrial revolution has come to carry connotations and to bear meanings that increasingly fail to 'save the phenomena'.

My main aim in the lectures was to question the appropriateness of the view that the industrial revolution was a cumulative, progressive, unitary phenomenon. Much writing about it reflects this assumption either explicitly or implicitly, but there are several considerations that tell strongly against this view, and these are developed in the body of the book. As a convenient expository device, I have leaned heavily on the writings of the classical economists to clarify the nature of the problem. The economic growth process that Adam Smith described was indeed a cumulative, progressive and unitary phenomenon, which embraced a variety of changes in political, legal and social structures and attitudes as well as economic change. But, for reasons cogently argued by Smith himself and his successors, the momentum of growth was to be expected to peter out after a time, arrested by changes endogenous to the growth process itself, and giving rise in due course to the supervention of the stationary state. Moreover, the classical economists were unanimous in doubting whether even the then prevailing level of real wages could be sustained indefinitely. Future falls were more probable than future rises. A steady and substantial improvement in real wages for the mass of the population was a utopian pipe-dream, not a possibility that a rational and well-informed man could plausibly entertain, however much he might wish to see it occur. Yet a sustained rise in real wages has come to be regarded as one of the key distinguishing features of the industrial revolution.

Clearly we are faced with a paradox. How could it be that the best informed contemporaries, who lived through the decades which, by the conventional chronology of later writing, included the early stages of the industrial revolution, and who concentrated their formidable intellectual powers upon the behaviour of the economy, should not merely have been unaware of the developments seen by later generations as heralding a new age, but should have strongly and explicitly rejected the possibility of the change which was later to be identified as its most salient, single characteristic? Was the industrial revolution like the biblical thief in the night, stealing up on contemporaries unwares?

The paradox disappears, and the views of the classical economists seem more easily justifiable, if, instead of regarding the industrial revolution as a unitary process in the traditional fashion, the growth taking place in the eighteenth and nineteenth centuries is seen as the product of two different sets of forces having only an accidental relationship to one another in the early stages of their overlap in time.

The consideration that caused the classical economists to exercise so much caution in assessing future growth was their thinking about the land. The surface area of the earth was indisputably incapable of expansion, as was any sub-category of the surface, such as cultivable land. At any given level of material technology what could be obtained from the land and put to human use, though not subject to a crude and simple upper limit, could be increased only by committing a rising quantity of labour and capital to secure each unit increase in output. The economic law of declining marginal returns was inescapable. The future was therefore bound to appear gloomy as long as it seemed proper to assume that the productivity of the land conditioned prospects, not merely for the supply of food in particular, but also for economic growth generally. Only if there were radical and continuous advances in agricultural technology could this fate be avoided, and none of the classical economists thought it reasonable to suppose that technological advance would meet such exacting requirements.

Viewing the future with concern, did not mean that *no* progress was possible or that the progress already made was insignificant. On the contrary, by creating an appropriate legal framework, fostering predictability in economic planning and action, protecting property rights, and securing the enforceability of contracts; by removing constraints on the use of capital and the freedom of labour; by ensuring that governments refrained from arbitrary taxation; by encouraging freedom of trade both internal and external, and thus furthering specialization of function, societies could liberate powers of production long frustrated and suppressed by the ineptness of feudal or mercantilist states. The wealth of nations could be much increased and the living standards of their populations raised by learning to work with the grain of human nature rather than against it.

There was no flaw in the general logic deployed by the classical economists. Their writings remain authoritative for the analysis of growth within the confines of a traditional economy, an economy bounded by the productivity of the land, what I shall term an organic economy. It escaped their notice, however, that a different economic base was emerging whose character contrasted sharply with that of any organic economy.

Some of the salient features of the new regime will be clear by implication from a description of the nature of the organic economy. It escaped from the problem of the fixed supply of land and of its organic products by using mineral raw materials. Thus the typical industries of the new regime produced iron, pottery, bricks, glass and inorganic chemicals, or secondary products made from such materials, above all an immense profusion of machines, tools and consumer products fashioned out of iron and steel. The expansion of such industries could continue to any scale without causing significant pressure on the land, whereas the major industries of an organic economy, textiles, leather and construction, for example, could only grow if more wool, hides or wood were produced which in turn implied the commitment of larger and larger acreages to such ends, and entailed fiercer and fiercer competition for a factor of production whose supply could not be increased. Meeting all basic human needs, for food, clothing, housing and fuel, inevitably meant mounting pressure on the same scarce resource.

But there were further features of the new regime whose nature was not implied by contrast with the nature of an organic economy, and which revised the prospects for future growth and a higher standard of living still more emphatically. All material production requires the expenditure of energy in the form of heat or mechanical work, and the level of productivity per man that can be reached is strongly conditioned by this, which in turn largely determines real wages and living standards. Quite apart form the depressing implications of the principle of declining marginal returns for living standards in an organic economy, such an economy was necessarily severely inhibited by its energy budget. Just as raw materials were almost all organic, both heat and mechanical energy were obtained from organic sources, the heat energy from burning wood (or its derivative charcoal); the mechanical energy from human or animal muscle. The latter in particular was a major influence limiting productivity, since many forms of production require mechanical energy on a large scale to perform the sequence of operations involved. The cultivation of the land or the working of metals are prime examples of this point. Productivity is necessarily low if human muscle alone is deployed to lift the spade or raise the hammer. Animal muscle may serve to raise productivity horizons where the horse or ox can be harnessed to the task, but the benefit, though substantial, is limited. Moreover, since animals need the same 'fuel' as men they compete with men for the same scarce resource, fertile land. When, therefore, a mineral source, coal, began to supply more and more of the heat energy needed by industry, and later, following the development of an effective device for turning heat into mechanical energy in the form of the steam engine, also provided a solution to the problem of securing a virtually unlimited supply of such power, the prospects for growth both in aggregate output and in output per head were entirely transformed from those which had always previously obtained.

The argument sketched here is developed at greater length in the body of this book. The book remains, however, an essay and not a treatise. My aim is not to try to establish a new orthodoxy. It is to reanimate interest in the events that brought into being a world of huge cities and an industrialized countryside; a world that no longer follows the rhythm of the sun and the seasons; a world in which the fortunes of man depend largely upon how he himself regulates the economy and not upon the vagaries of weather and harvest; a world in which poverty has become an optional state rather than a reflection of the necessary limitations of human productive powers; a world increasingly free from major natural disasters but in which human folly can mean utter and total destruction; a world that has gained an awesome momentum of growth but may lose any semblance of stability. Such has been the legacy of the industrial revolution. It repays closer study both because of its intrinsic fascination and to assist us in knowing ourselves. We cannot choose but to be the inheritors of the industrial revolution; we can choose to know our inheritance better than we do.

1

Definitions and concepts

In the mid-sixteenth century England's peripheral location at the edge of continental Europe was symbolically appropriate both demographically and economically. The island was relatively sparsely peopled. Her population was only a fifth that of France, or about a quarter that of Germany or Italy.[1] In agriculture, industry and commerce advance depended heavily on the importation from the continent of more sophisticated techniques. It could be argued that by the late twentieth century in economic matters the ancient pattern had re-established itself; that the wheel has turned full circle; that in one sense of the term a revolution had occurred. Whatever the truth of this view, there can be no dispute that in the interim a revolution in another sense of the term had taken place, nor that it has transformed the economic, social and demographic constitution of countries across the face of the globe more profoundly than any other change in the history of literate societies. Furthermore, this other revolution, in its initial stages, was largely played out in England and the other countries of the British Isles, a fact which might naturally cause British historians to devote to it particular attention.

The industrial revolution is the centrepiece of world history over recent centuries, and *a fortiori* of the country in which it began. Yet its significance, though seldom denied, is not prominently visible in general historical writing. It is almost as if the very bulk of the phenomenon had either rendered it invisible, absorbing it into the

[1] Wrigley, 'The growth of population in eighteenth-century England', pp. 121–2.

backcloth of the stage, or had made it too formidable an object to be confronted face to face. To the generalist historian the technicalities of the subject are forbidding. To most economists, with their eyes on the present, it is too distant in time to command attention. Even to economic historians, for whom the study of the industrial revolution might be expected to be in some sense their *raison d'être*, the topic is often uninspiring, or has become fragmented into a series of specialisms so that individual trees may receive painstaking attention but the familiar mass of the wood is favoured only with a passing glance. Although the world today has been made over in its image, the industrial revolution, astonishingly, often manages to appear a dull topic. By directing attention to some aspects of the received wisdom concerning the industrial revolution which are in need of reconsideration, I hope to promote discussion of the wider issues involved and to reawaken a sense of excitement about its fascination and importance.

The industrial revolution: defining the concept

It is convenient to begin with the term itself. Both the adjective and the noun, but particularly the two in conjunction, can prove obstacles to the better understanding of the changes which occurred. The adjective 'industrial' may appear to exclude agriculture and commerce, or at least to relegate them to a less important role within the period of change, while the noun 'revolution' is apt, by analogy with its use in political contexts, to suggest rapid change from one relatively stable system to another, as in passing from an absolutist to a democratic state. Moreover, when the two words are juxtaposed as 'industrial revolution', a presumption is created that the process is unitary and progressive, so that once in train it is impelled by a necessary logic to conform to a particular pattern. Such a presumption can be damaging to an informed discussion of the chronology, course and cause of the phenomenon.

If the use of the term 'industrial revolution' does indeed tend to promote assumptions of this sort, its universal currency is unfortunate. Between Tudor and Victorian times there were very remarkable changes in English agriculture and commerce. Indeed, it is probable that productivity changes were more striking in these two aspects of economic life than in industry over most of the quarter millennium separating the reigns of Elizabeth and Victoria.[2] Again, it is highly misleading to suppose that before and after the industrial revolution there were periods of comparative stasis separated by a period of feverish change. That the twentieth century has remained a period of rapid change needs little emphasis, but it is almost equally mistaken to view the period preceding the industrial revolution as characterized by relatively little change. Nor is it satisfactory to be trapped by terminology into regarding the industrial revolution as a unitary and progressive phenomenon, especially if the conventional chronology is accepted whereby it began about 1780 and had already reached a degreee of maturity by, say, 1830. Until the latter date, or perhaps even later, such growth as occurred may be better viewed as an extension of growth with a very long pedigree; only thereafter was the momentum of growth increasingly sustained by novel forces.

It will already be apparent that in spite of my reservations about the term 'industrial revolution', I have not chosen to forego its use.[3] It may probably be regarded as too deeply rooted in thought and usage to be supplanted. I will, however, suggest a definition of its meaning which will govern my subsequent use of the term in the hope of reducing the customary imprecision with which it is used. And I shall introduce some supplementary terms to try to clarify both the nature and the periodization of the growth which took place.

The distinguishing feature of the industrial revolution which has transformed the lives of the inhabitants of industrialized societies has been a large and sustained rise in real incomes per head. Without such a change the bulk of all income would necessarily have con-

---

[2] See below pp. 35–6, 81–7, 126–31.

[3] Both Mokyr and Crafts have recently expressed reservations about the use of the term but have concluded that it is too deeply embedded in common parlance to attempt to effect a change. Mokyr provides an interesting reflection on its nature. 'Examining British economic history in the period 1760–1830 is a bit like studying the history of the Jewish dissenters between 50 B.C. and 50 A.D. What we are looking at is the inception of something which was at first insignificant and even bizarre, but destined to change the life of every man and woman in the West, and strongly affect the lives of others even though the phenomenon remained confined primarily to Europe and its offshoots.' Crafts, British economic growth, p. 6; Mokyr, 'The industrial revolution and the New Economic History', pp. 3–4, 44.

tinued to be spent on food and the bulk of the labour force would therefore have continued to be employed upon the land.[4] Only in the wake of rising output per head, the twin of increasing real incomes, were major shifts in the structure of demand conceivable, and in sympathy with such shifts, matching changes in occupational structure; progressive urbanization; and the host of associated changes comprising the industrial revolution. To define economic growth in this way is not new. It is in essence the definition adopted by Adam Smith on the opening page of the *Wealth of nations*.[5] It does, however, entail a different perspective on the phenomenon as a whole from that often apprehended from the term industrial revolution. For example, by directing attention to increases in productivity, it avoids any danger of supposing that the critical changes were necessarily those taking place in industry. And, by employing what is in essence a ratio measure as the criterion of success, it should ensure that trends in population no less than trends in output are taken into account.[6] A doubling of production matched by a doubling in

[4]   Recent data for a scattering of developed and developing countries, ranging from the United States to Nigeria, suggest a close linear relationship between the proportion of the workforce engaged in agriculture and the percentage of income spent on food. Hall, 'The role of energy', fig. 5, p. 51.

[5]   'The annual labour of every nation is the fund which originally supplies it with all the necessaries and conveniencies of life which it annually consumes, and which is always either in the immediate produce of that labour, or in what is purchased with that produce from other nations. According, therefore, as this produce or what is purchased with it bears a greater or smaller proportion to the number of those who are to consume it, the nation will be better or worse supplied with all the necessaries and conveniencies for which it has occasion.' Smith, *Wealth of nations*, ed. Cannan, I, p. 1.

[6]   Population questions have not normally received very much attention from economists or even from economic historians, and yet as Schumpeter remarked: 'The problems of population, that is to say the question what it is that determines the size of human societies and what the consequences are that attend the increase or decrease in the number of a country's inhabitants, might well be the first to occur to a perfectly detached observer as soon as he looks at those societies in a spirit of scientific curiosity. The view that the key to historical processes is to be found in the variations of populations, though one-sided, is at least as reasonable as is any other theory of history that proceeds from the prejudice that there must be a single prime mover of social or economic evolution – such as technology, race, class struggle, capital formation, and what not.' Schumpeter, *History of economic analysis*, p. 250.

numbers represents a substantial growth in aggregate output but no improvement in productivity. Only when output growth exceeds population increase substantially and consistently can there be grounds for supposing that an industrial revolution is in train.

Defining the concept of an industrial revolution in this way also immediately brings to light a difficulty with the traditional chronology of the industrial revolution in England, for there is greater uncertainty about the trend in real income per head for the mass of the population in the period 1780-1830, often taken to be the springtime of the industrial revolution, than in either the preceding or succeeding century. In the earlier and later periods there can be no reasonable doubt that real incomes per head increased substantially; in the middle period any advance was less clear cut, and may well have been confined to certain groups within the population.[7]

At this point it may prove helpful to rehearse briefly the line of argument that I intend to develop about the problems of understanding the industrial revolution in England. This will occupy the balance of this first chapter. Later I shall provide some supporting evidence for the thesis advanced and offer some reflections on the implications of my approach for the existing 'models' of the industrial revolution.

Given the continued strength of the presumption that the break with a pre-industrial past began sometime in the middle or later decades of the eighteenth century, it is important to begin by stressing the extent to which economic activity in England had already drifted away from the prevailing norm in continental western Europe during the seventeenth and eighteenth centuries. Indeed, one of the casualties of any informed reassessment of the industrial revolution as an historical phenomenon should be the view that it was a unitary, progressive series of events taking place over a restricted time scale. The transformation that gave rise to the industrial revolution is better regarded as spread over a period lasting more

---

[7] See, for example, Flinn, 'Trends in real wages'; von Tunzelmann, 'Trends in real wages revisited'; Lindert and Williamson, 'English workers' living standards'. Evidence of substantial regional disparities in real wage trends and of continued upward movement in some industrializing areas in the north, may be found in Hunt, 'Industrialization and regional inequality', and Botham and Hunt, 'Wages during the industrial revolution'.

than two centuries, and consisting of two main component types of economic growth so markedly dissimilar in nature and with such different chronology that it is questionable whether their under-standing is well served by using a single umbrella term to describe them; perhaps the course of change would be more easily and acc-urately understood if they were more clearly distinguished and the industrial revolution were regarded as their joint product.

It is implicit in the latter view that it is misleading to suppose that the development of one component type out of the other was in some sense preordained, that the second developed ineluctably out of the first. From a stance in the twentieth century the transition from one to the other may appear smooth and inevitable. It was unanticipated by contemporaries, however, and there is much to be learnt from the arguments that they advanced which imply that what actually occurred was extremely improbable, or even flatly impossible.

The first of the two types of economic growth is associated with what I shall term the advanced organic economy; the second with the mineral-based energy economy. The former precedes the latter in time, though there is overlap between them. Each is a stereotype, of value for conceptual clarity, but never encountered in a pure form in the empirical complexity of history. The reason for the choice of these inelegant, cumbersome names should appear as the argument develops and will be discussed explicitly at a later stage.

The growth surge in England in the seventeenth and eighteenth centuries

The extent of the economic advance of England between c. 1550 and c. 1800, both in absolute terms, and relative to other countries in western Europe, is not hard to demonstrate. It is, for example, reflec-ted in the striking changes in the occupational structure of the labour force. At the former date the great bulk of the population lived in the countryside and made a living by work on the land. By the latter date although the majority of the population still lived in rural areas, only about 40 per cent of the adult male labour force worked in agriculture, the lowest percentage of any European country. Else-where in Europe any fall in the proportion of the labour force engaged in agriculture was much more modest: between 60 and 80 per cent of the adult male labour force still worked on the land in 1800.[8]

In Elizabethan times England was less urbanized than the average of west European countries. Georgian England, in contrast, was the most highly urbanized of all European countries, with the exception of The Netherlands. Moreover, urban growth was taking place at such a formidable pace that about 70 per cent of all European urban growth was taking place in England alone during the second half of the eighteenth century.[9] In The Netherlands, in contrast, the eighteenth century was a period of urban decline.[10] London, always by far the largest city in England, was not in the European 'top ten' in 1550. By the end of the seventeenth century it had become the largest city in Europe, and thereafter easily sustained its supremacy.[11]

In no other major country of western Europe did population growth approach the pace found in England. Between 1550 and 1820 the populations of France, Spain, Germany, Italy and The Netherlands all appear to have grown by between 50 and 80 per cent; in England over the same period the comparable figure was 280 per cent, a contrast so striking that by 1820 England, which had once been a small country by the standards of the larger European powers, though still less populous than France, Germany or Italy, was moving rapidly towards rough equality with them.[12] Yet, so far as the comparison can be made with propriety, it is probably right to suppose that real incomes per head were higher in England in 1800 than anywhere else in Europe. In the late seventeenth century, in contrast, real incomes in The Netherlands, then the most advanced economy in Europe, have recently been estimated to have been at least 50 per cent higher than in England.[13]

[8] Some data on agricultural employment in continental European countries may be found in Wrigley, 'Urban growth and agricultural change', p. 163 n. 32. For English data, see Wrigley, 'Men on the land', tab. 11.12, p. 322.

[9] Wrigley, 'Urban growth and agricultural change', tab. 7, p. 149.

[10] Ibid., tab. 8, p. 154.

[11] For comparative information about the size and rank order of European cities, see de Vries, *European urbanization*, esp. chs. 3 and 4, and app. 1.

[12] Wrigley, 'The growth of population in eighteenth-century England', pp. 122–3.

[13] De Vries, 'Decline and rise of the Dutch economy', fig. 8, p. 184.

Simple arithmetic suggests that if population growth was so much faster in England than elsewhere while the standard of living was rising substantially relative to that in other countries, the contrast in rates of growth in gross national product must have been even more striking.

The most significant feature of English economic history in the seventeenth and eighteenth centuries, serving in some sense to 'explain' her notable general success relative to other European countries, was the advance achieved in productivity per head in agriculture. Once again simple arithmetic captures the essence of the matter. A combination of empirical evidence and general considerations makes it plausible to suppose that the labour force engaged in agriculture was little if any larger in 1800 than it had been 200 years earlier, even though the population had more than doubled in the interim. Yet at both dates England was broadly self-sufficient in basic foodstuffs. Since there is little reason to think that food intake per head was significantly less in 1800 than in 1600, or that the average diet was more restricted, it follows that output per head in agriculture must have roughly doubled. It is also demonstrable that the change was achieved principally through increased output per acre rather than by breaking in large tracts of new land. The contrast with the continent is again notable. Similar calculations to those just presented for England, for example, suggest that in France output per head in agriculture rose much more modestly, by perhaps 20 per cent. Again, whereas output of wheat per acre in England at the end of the eighteenth century was roughly double that in France, in the sixteenth century there was probably little difference between the two countries in this respect.[14]

The combination of a largely static agricultural labour force and rapid population growth implies, of course, a particularly swift growth in non-agricultural employment. Once again English experience represents a marked contrast to that elsewhere in Europe, not just in that the rate of growth of employment outside agriculture was so much higher than elsewhere, but in a structural sense. The painstaking work of de Vries has recently demonstrated that in

[14] Wrigley, 'Urban growth and agricultural change', tab. 4, pp. 140–1, tab. 10, p. 160; also Wrigley, 'Corn yields and prices', p. 97 n. 13 and p. 128 n. 54 for sources and data on wheat yields.

Europe as a whole between about 1500 and 1750 urban growth was largely confined to a small number of large cities. Cities whose population was less than 40,000 barely kept pace with the overall growth in population during this long period.[15] De Vries views this phenomenon as the joint product of the loss of local autonomy and political power by small urban centres and of the growth of industry in the countryside, especially in the form often termed proto-indu-strial.[16] But in England the pattern was different. There was indeed a very rapid growth in rural employment outside agriculture, in handicraft industry, mining, transport and service occupations, but this did not occur at the expense of vigorous urban expansion. Towns in all size categories grew at a broadly similar rate in the seventeenth and eighteenth centuries, and there were large increases in the number of towns in each size category. On the continent the number of towns with between 5,000 and 10,000 inhabitants actually fell between 1600 and 1750; in England the number doubled.[17] Well might Adam Smith refer to the exchange between town and country as 'the great commerce of every civilized society',[18] when reflecting on the English experience of growth. Urban growth and agricultural prosperity were intimately connected and mutually stimulating, as he emphasized strongly.

The contrast between England and the continent in urban growth patterns extends further. In continental countries lists of the ten or twenty largest towns in 1800 consist of substantially the same names as comparable lists for 1600, and usually with only minor changes in the rank ordering of the towns.[19] In England very striking changes took place over the same time period. London was at all times by far the largest city, but of the next nine in 1600 only four also appear on the list for 1800. At that date Manchester, Liverpool and Birmingham, all newcomers, were second, third and fourth. Then came Bristol, which was on the earlier list, but sixth and seventh were two further newcomers, Leeds and Sheffield, so that

---

[15] De Vries, 'Patterns of urbanization', pp. 94–6.
[16] De Vries, *European urbanization*, pp. 238–46.
[17] Wrigley, 'Urban growth and agricultural change', p. 151.
[18] Smith, *Wealth of nations*, ed. Cannan, I, p. 401.
[19] The basic data for the exercise are available in de Vries, *European urbanization*, app. 1. See also Chandler and Fox, *Urban growth*.

five of the six largest towns after London in 1800 had been relatively unimportant centres two centuries earlier.[20]

Ministers of state and entrepreneurs in the reign of Elizabeth, if they were intent upon the introduction of new industries, or of new methods of production, of new crops, or of new types of cultivation, of improvements in transport, or of more sophisticated techniques of book-keeping or credit transfer, almost always looked to the continent for information and instruction.[21] Two hundred years later the pattern was reversed.

Relative to her neighbours and rivals, therefore, England in the seventeenth and eighteenth centuries was making rapid economic progress. Whether addressed through the consideration of aggregate growth, structural change, technical advance or income per head, substantial and in some cases spectacular relative improvement is visible. It is probably also justifiable to assert that the gap was widening steadily down to the early nineteenth century. Contrast this with the position a century later. Although in the conventional view of its chronology, the industrial revolution was principally a nineteenth-century phenomenon, and is depicted as the reason for a period of British economic hegemony, by about 1900 it was clear to contemporaries, and is demonstrable in many quantitative series, that her new rivals, Germany and the United States, had overtaken or were about to overtake her, and that a following pack of other countries was also rapidly cutting into any lead which Britain might still possess. In terms of all the categories used previously, aggregate growth, structural change, technical advance and income per head, any remaining British advantage was slight or declining. In some cases a reverse gap had already appeared.

To the degree that this is a fair reading of the economic history of three centuries, it suggests an intriguing paradox. In the period before the conventional industrial revolution the English economy was remarkably successful relative to other European countries. No sooner had the industrial revolution taken place than the relative success began to evaporate, even though absolute progress continued, and indeed grew swifter. How can this paradox be resolved?

[20] Wrigley, 'Urban growth and agricultural change', tab. 1, pp. 126–7.
[21] See, for example, the many illustrations of the point in Thirsk, *Economic policy and projects*.

Can it be true that the event which is supposed to epitomize English economic success also signalled the rapid approach of the moment when her economic dominance was to be extinguished?

Two modes of economic growth

The essence of the matter can be put quite succinctly, and involves recourse to the distinction already mentioned. The period down to the early nineteenth century may be regarded as a period in which the sources of growth were mainly those of an advanced organic economy. Thereafter the mineral-based energy economy was increasingly dominant as the vehicle of growth. Of course there was a substantial overlap in time between the two but it is convenient to begin by oversimplifying in order to establish the contrasts between them.

The nature of the earlier system is depicted with great clarity in the writings of the classical economists. Their success in this regard is indeed the most notable of all the attempts to create an intellectual structure capable of giving insight into the functioning of the type of socio-economic system prevailing in early modern England.

Within the canons of the system constructed by the classical economists the opportunity for growth was very substantial but yet firmly limited. The parable of the pinmakers provided an illustration of the way in which huge increases both in aggregate output and in individual productivity could be achieved. The interconnections between market size, transport provision, commercial sophistication and specialization of function were laid bare. The links between the exercise of rational self-interest and public advantage were examined. The key role of government in providing security of the person and possessions; in fostering predictability within a suitable legal system; and, not least, in refraining from actions such as arbitrary measures of taxation or ill-advised interference in economic affairs was explained. But growth was nonetheless regarded as severely and inescapably limited by the fact that one of the triad of factors – land, labour and capital – upon whose combination all production depended, was in fixed supply. The land surface of the earth could not be increased and for this reason the impact of declining marginal returns in agriculture, though capable of postponement, could not in the long run be avoided.[22]

To the modern eye identifying land as one of the three basic factors of production may seem excessively restrictive, and, in consequence, inasmuch as the term remains in use in this connection, it is often interpreted to include much more than the land *sensu stricto*. But it was proper to take it literally in reference to the early modern economy since the land was not simply the principal source of food for the population, but also virtually the sole source of the raw materials used in industrial production. Those not employed in agriculture were chiefly engaged in processing animal or vegetable products. Spinners and weavers, fullers and dyers; tanners and curriers; tailors and shoemakers; sawyers, coopers, carpenters and cabinetmakers: trades such as these made up the bulk of industrial employment. Wool, flax, silk, cotton, hides, leather, hair, fur, straw, wood: these were the prime raw materials of manufacturing industry. The building industry was less exclusively confined to organic raw materials than most others, but remained heavily dependent on wood. Wood was also the prime source of the heat energy needed in innumerable industrial and domestic activities.

There were some men whose livelihood was not thus tied to the output of the land, such as miners or masons. But even those workers whose output consisted of metals fashioned to various human needs – smiths of all types, for instance – were dependent on the productivity of the land for the scale of their output, because a vegetable material, charcoal in this instance, was necessary as a source of heat for smelting and working the metal if the crude ores were to be rendered into pewter mugs, iron ploughshares or brass candlesticks. An iron industry was as likely to founder because the need for charcoal had denuded the local forest cover as because local ores had become exhausted. Again, since many branches of industry, most mining ventures and almost all forms of transport, as well as agriculture, made extensive use of animal muscle as a source of mechanical energy, the productivity of the land was crucial to the supply of power as well as heat. Woodland and pasture were as

[22] The view of the writings of the classical economists that is described in this section
      may be found in a more fully developed form in Wrigley, 'The classical economists
      and the industrial revolution'.

necessary to English industry as her arable land was to the family table.

A recognition of the significance of the productivity of the land to the whole range of the productive activities of society is both implicit and explicit in the writings of the classical economists, and the leverage which the application of the principle of declining marginal returns thus exerted was very powerful. As population and production expanded, the demands made upon the land were certain to rise at least *pari passu*.[23] Either this must mean taking new and poorer land into use, or coaxing a larger output from the land already in cultivation, or, more probably, some combination of the two. Unless there were offsetting advances in production techniques, larger and larger inputs of capital and labour would be needed to produce a unit increase in output. This in turn led, through declining returns on capital and hence a reduced incentive to invest, to the supervention of the 'stationary state', a key concept from Adam Smith to John Stuart Mill, and one invested with uninviting characteristics by those who pursued the implications of declining marginal returns to their logical conclusion.[24]

All growth was therefore limited growth, almost one might say conditional growth, made the more uncertain by the pressures which might arise from the behaviour of another member of the triad of basic economic factors. It was Malthus who brought this aspect of the matter most vividly into focus, though his treatment of the issue is foreshadowed in the *Wealth of nations*. The supply of labour is a function of population movements. Adam Smith had supposed that population danced to a tune played by the demand for labour. He was confident that the high fertility of labourers and artisans ensured that high growth potential was ever present but the degree to which it was realized was determined by the relative prosperity of the times. When demand for labour was brisk, employment

---

[23] Ibid., pp. 26–9.

[24] These issues are discussed at greater length in Wrigley, 'The limits to growth: Malthus and the classical economists'. Deane remarked, 'The most distinctive feature of classical growth theory was that it came to see the growth process as an inexorable movement in the direction of a stationary state. The argument rests essentially on the Malthusian population principle (already foreshadowed by Smith) and the law of historically diminishing returns.' Deane, *Evolution of economic ideas*, p. 37.

available and wages comparatively high, the common people ate well and their children survived. In poorer times, more children died. He did not, however, enter into the subject very fully, no doubt convinced that the truth of his assertions was virtually self-evident.[25]

Malthus first discussed the matter in a remarkable brief treatise, perhaps best described as a lengthy and brilliant pamphlet, the first *Essay on population*.[26] In the second and subsequent editions he greatly elaborated and substantially modified his first thoughts, arguing that the living standards of the mass of the population at all times, but especially on the approach of the stationary state, were strongly influenced by the demographic regime prevailing. At one extreme stood the 'Chinese' case, where the mass of the population was accustomed to exist on a pittance, and lived in a society which gave strong, unconditional support to early marriage.[27] In such a society many lived close to the precipice and were easily pushed over the edge by a poor harvest or a surge in food prices, however produced. At the other extreme was the pattern best exemplified in parts of western Europe. Here conventions existed and were observed that prescribed relatively high minimum living standards, and their effectiveness was secured by appropriate marriage customs. Couples were reluctant to embark upon marriage or might refrain from it entirely when times were unpromising. Marriage was not triggered by the approach or attainment of sexual maturity in young women as elsewhere but was governed by economic circumstances. As a result, not only was fertility always lower than in other cultures, but it could be adjusted to suit the prevailing economic climate.[28]

---

[25] Smith, *Wealth of nations*, ed. Cannan, I, pp. 88–90.

[26] Malthus, *Essay on population* (1798).

[27] 'The labourers of the south of England are so accustomed to eat fine wheaten bread, that they will suffer themselves to be half starved, before they will submit to live like the Scottish peasants. They might perhaps in time, by the operation of the hard law of necessity be reduced to live even like the lower Chinese.' Ibid., p. 49.

[28] Having described the severity of the pressure of population in China, and its bitter consequences, Malthus turned to a brief sketch of the restraints upon marriage in England which he took as an example of Europe more generally, describing how each major social group was affected somewhat differently. Ibid., pp. 26–8. The whole issue was, of course, examined much more fully in the later editions of the *Essay on population*.

The significance of the distinction is perhaps most easily grasped by setting it out diagramatically. In the upper panel of figure 1.1 the line labelled M shows how mortality rises from a base level set by the local disease environment. When population size increases beyond a certain point pressure upon food supplies begins to be experienced. Thereafter mortality (M) rises steadily with further population growth. If fertility is high and invariant (F_1 – the 'Chinese' case), population growth will cease only when numbers have reached a high total. The implication for living standards of the existence of a large population is made clear in the lower panel of the figure where the population, P_1, produced by high fertility and high mortality

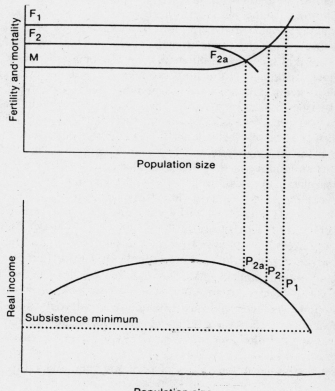

Figure 1.1
Fertility, mortality and living standards

must in consequence cope with low real incomes. If fertility is generally lower (F_2) population growth, *ceteris paribus*, ceases at a lower
point with significant benefit to living standards (P_2). Such a situation may arise simply from later marriage and the lower fertility that
will accompany delayed marriage in populations not practising contraception. If fertility is both generally lower and in addition sensitive
to an increased pressure on living standards, as when the decision to
marry or to refrain from marriage is taken with an eye to economic
circumstances and prospects (F_{2a}), the population will find itself still
further removed from the edge of the precipice and a modest prosperity may be widely diffused (P_{2a}).

Malthus's identification of the importance of a social aspect of
community behaviour which might prove as important as any
economic variable in determining living standards gave a new
dimension to the consideration of the question of both the level and
trend of real incomes. Population is the denominator where aggregate production is the numerator in the ratio which decides
whether living standards are high, and the relative growth paths of
the two jointly determine trends in living standards. Periodic secular
fluctuations in living standards are a structural feature of Malthus's
model of economic behaviour (he termed them 'oscillations').[29]
Where the marriage system and prevailing norms of behaviour permitted an improvement in living standards during the upswing of
the oscillation to be retained and consolidated in the form of a higher
conventional living standard, rather than being eroded by a move to
earlier marriage encouraged by the easier economic climate, the
possibility of a secular rise in living standards existed.[30] Similar,
ratchet-like behaviour over several successive cycles might in principle advance living standards substantially over the centuries.

In elaborating this topic Malthus both identified the reason why
the west European marriage system was capable of producing
profound differences between the economic characteristics of Europe
and of other parts of the world, and added a new dimension to the
debate about the long-term prospects for living standards. In a Ricar-
dian world only technical innovation in agriculture could delay the
onset of the deleterious effect of declining marginal returns on

[29] Ibid., pp. 14–15.
[30] Malthus, *Principles of political economy*, v, pp. 183–4.

standards of living and growth prospects.[31] In a Malthusian world a society able and willing to control its fertility by appropriate marriage behaviour could arrest or even reverse any incipient slide in real incomes by ensuring that the ratio of population to production remained favourable. Population trends are not solely dependent upon economic pressures in a Malthusian system, or perhaps it would be more accurate to say that the pressures are so mediated by the socio-demographic system as to create a wide range of possible outcomes rather than an inevitable tendency towards a stationary state in which real incomes are both low and under constant pressure, as was the case in Ricardo's analysis.

Though the writings of the classical economists throw much light on the growth process in early modern England, however, they do not suggest how an advanced organic system might ultimately itself be replaced. It is an implicit assumption in their writings that the constraints imposed by a universal dependence on organic raw materials were severe and permanent. A particular agrarian system, with landlords, tenant farmers and labourers rather than, say, peasants and manorial lords, might have allowed England to make striking progress in agricultural productivity. A marriage system in which female age at marriage was governed by economic events rather than biological maturation might have brought major benefits to western Europe compared with extra-European cultures where it was shameful for any woman to pass beyond menarche unmarried. But these were variations upon the same basic theme, not notes comprising a completely new tune being picked out for the first time in late Georgian England.

This view remained common until a surprisingly late date.[32] John

[31] Ricardo, *Principles of political economy*, pp. 119–21.

[32] Though, inevitably, a consciousness of the changed circumstances of production caused the classical assumptions to be more and more widely questioned. It is instructive, for example, to note that McCulloch in his edition of the *Wealth of nations* added a scathing footnote to Adam Smith's argument that the employment capital in agriculture was 'by far the most advantageous to the society' of all the ways in which it could be employed. 'This is perhaps the most objectionable passage in the *Wealth of nations*', McCulloch wrote, 'and it is really astonishing so acute and sagacious a reasoner as Dr Smith should have maintained a proposition so manifestly erroneous as that "*nature does nothing for man in manufacture.*" The powers of water and of wind, which move our machinery, support our ships, and impel them over the deep – the pressure of the atmosphere and the elasticity of steam, which enable us to work the most stupendous engines – are they not the spontaneous gifts of nature?' Smith, *Wealth of nations*, ed. McCulloch, p. 162n.

Stuart Mill, a bell-wether figure, and very widely read, was unsure about future prospects and about the severity of constraints upon growth in output per head. Writing in the third quarter of the nineteenth century (the first edition of the *Principles of economics* was published in 1848 and there were several subsequent editions before his death in 1873), Mill remarked,

The materials of manufacture being all drawn from the land, and many of them from agriculture, which supplies in particular the entire material of clothing; the general law of production from the land, the law of diminishing return, must in the last resort be applicable to manufacturing as well as to agricultural history. As population increases, and the power of the land to yield increased produce is strained harder and harder, any additional supply of material, as well as of food, must be obtained by a more than proportionally increasing expenditure of labour.[33]

However, because the cost of raw materials was normally only a small part of total factor cost in manufacturing, and labour productivity could be greatly raised by mechanical aids and the division of labour, the general outcome was uncertain:

It is quite conceivable that the efficiency of agricultural labour might be undergoing, with the increase of produce, a gradual diminution; that the price of food, in consequence, might be progressively rising, and an ever growing proportion of the population might be needed to raise food for the whole; while yet the productive power of labour in all other branches of industry might be so rapidly augmenting, that the required amount of labour could be spared for manufactures, and nevertheless a greater produce be obtained and the aggregate wants of the community be on the whole better supplied, than before.[34]

Mill remained unsure about the secular prospect for the living standards of the mass of the population. On the one hand he expected the advent at some point of the stationary state, and was dubious about the prospects for the real incomes of the mass of the population, following Malthus in arguing that restraint upon fertility was the surest way of securing an enhancement in the living standards

[33] Mill, *Principles of political economy*, I, p. 182.
[34] Ibid., p. 182.

of the labouring masses.[35] On the other hand he argued that because raw material costs were only a small fraction of total factor costs of production in most manufacturing industries, and because *increasing* returns to labour inputs were readily obtainable in manufacturing, the problems associated with dependence on the produce of the land could be overcome at least for the foreseeable future. The radical nature of the change in the basis of economic growth then in train escaped him.

The nature of the change from an advanced organic to a mineral-based energy economy may be simply expressed, and is, indeed, implicit in the terms used. Its implications, however, run wide and deep. To escape from the constraints of the principle of diminishing returns, it is necessary to find substitutes for animal and vegetable raw materials in production processes, and substitutes, moreover, which do not suffer from the same disadvantage. To Mill, who lived, of course, at a time when the increasing importance of mineral raw materials was unmistakable, an increasing dependence on mineral raw materials was like jumping out of the frying pan into the fire. The extraction of minerals was just as much subject to the problem of declining marginal returns as the production of wheat or wool, but with the additional problem that every ton of coal or iron ore dug from the ground was a ton less available to be extracted at a later date, a restriction from which agricultural production was free.

To view the matter in this fashion, however, does not do justice to it. It is true that, to use canonist terminology, the land is a fungible, whereas minerals are consumptibles. The one is valueless apart from its consumption, where the other may be used repeatedly and yet retain its worth. And it is also true that over a sufficiently long period of time the added disadvantage to which Mill made reference implies a special danger in increasing dependence upon consumptibles, as

---

[35] See, for example, the arguments presented in ibid., pp. 340–6. Mill expressed grave doubts about the willingness of agricultural labourers to practise any prudential restraint, though he was more optimistic about skilled artisans and the middle classes. He was quite clear that, apart from new colonies, 'it is impossible that population should increase at its utmost rate without lowering wages', and feared that labourers, provided with an adventitious increase in wages, would fail to protect it. 'If they content themselves with enjoying the greater comfort while it lasts, but do not learn to require it, they will people down to their old scale of living.' Ibid., pp. 342, 345.

the recent history of oil production and prices has demonstrated. But it must be borne in mind that, precisely because coal, for example, is a consumptible, the absolute scale of production may be much more easily capable of expansion at constant or falling unit costs of production than is feasible with the production of wood. A thousand acres of woodland will yield, say, 1,000 tons of wood each year for an indefinite period, but if production is increased to 2,000 tons the higher production level can only be maintained for a limited period as the timber capital available in the standing trees is rapidly reduced towards zero. Thereafter production must revert, at best, to its earlier, sustainable level of output. The price of rapid expansion today will be penury tomorrow. True, no mine, however rich, can yield even 1,000 tons of coal a year without any limit of time. At such a modest level of output the day of exhaustion may be far distant but it will eventually dawn. But, equally, enormous increases in output may be secured for a substantial period in a way which has no parallel in the felling of timber. All depends on the ratio of required output to the scale of available deposits. Guano proved an excellent fertilizer, but the annual demand for guano, even from a small country like England, rapidly rose to the point where each year's demand involved quarrying a substantial proportion of the limited accumulations of bird dung. The span of time during which guano could be dug was therefore brief. In the case of coal, in contrast, although annual demand came to be measured in tens of millions of tons, even eventually in hundreds of millions, the scale of accessible deposits proved to be so vast that the ratio of annual demand to readily accessible deposits was comparatively small. For practical purposes, output of some mineral raw materials was free from the trammels found in trying to expand output from the land.

Given a favourable ratio between potential demand and accessible supply, therefore, a switch from organic to mineral raw materials may render irrelevant the consideration which was most powerful in persuading the classical economists that the prudent man must be a pessimist; provided, of course, that a steadily widening sector of total demand could be satisfied with products derived from the use of mineral rather than organic materials.

Before examining this issue further, however, it is appropriate to call attention to a related issue, perhaps of even greater significance to the understanding of the industrial revolution, closely linked to what has just been discussed, and also curiously neglected by the classical economists.

They had discussed at great length the productivity gains available to industry from specialization of function, linked to expanding demand and wider access to markets. They had also pointed to the significance of improved machinery and of advances in the techniques of production in the same context.[36] But the singular importance of the scale of energy use per worker, and of the development of new sources of energy, received much less attention. Yet, in relation to the phenomenon of the industrial revolution, the issue of the availability of new sources of heat energy and mechanical energy is fundamental. It is also a topic with very close links to the question of the escape from dependence on organic sources of raw material supply.[37]

The scale of output that a worker can achieve is heavily conditioned by the amount of power at his elbow. The differences between the area prepared for sowing by a man working with a spade, a man with a horse-drawn ploughteam and a man with a tractor and multiple plough is large at each successive step. The same is true for the quantity of thread spun per worker using a distaff, tending a water-powered mule and working in a ring-spinning shed. In transport there are comparable gradations in productivity between economies where wheelbarrows, horse-drawn waggons and diesel-engined lorries are used to move goods. In the earlier of the two phases of economic history under review, the advanced organic phase, the great bulk of power used in most production processes was derived from organic sources. Human or animal muscle, supplemented for some purposes by wind or water power, was the prime mover for most agricultural, industrial and transport operations. Men did indeed live by the sweat of their brows.

[36] Adam Smith indeed had linked growing market size and the development of specialization of function to the appearance of a class of men who would make their living from inventing better machinery: 'philosophers or men of speculation, whose trade it is not to do any thing, but to observe everything; and who, upon that account, are often capable of combining together the powers of the most distant and dissimilar objects'. Smith, *Wealth of nations*, ed. Cannan, I, p. 14.

[37] Wrigley, 'Raw materials in the industrial revolution'.

Much of the heat needed in a wide variety of manufacturing processes also came from an organic source, in this case from wood. Power derived from organic sources was relatively small in scale, expensive and often not dependable. Even the stagecoach, the acme of achievement in swift land carriage, moved at the speed of a moderate cyclist. It was drawn by a yoke of four horses. Given that a working horse requires 3 to 5 acres for its sustenance, and that there was intense competition for the use of cultivable land, it is not surprising that travelling by stagecoach was an expensive business.

If in the course of a day's work a healthy man can prepare only a modest area for sowing; turn only a small quantity of leather into shoes; weave only a limited yardage of cloth, it is outside the power of ingenuity, benevolence or coercion to lift the burden of poverty from the bulk of the population. No matter how far specialization of function might be taken, or indeed how ingenious were the tools or mechanical devices employed in manufacture, the levels of productivity attainable across wide tracts of economic activity were necessarily quite modest as long as the main sources of power and heat were organic. The horizons of average individual productivity and, in parallel, of real incomes per head, therefore changed substantially when a switch to mineral sources of power and heat took place. Specialization growth had given way to power growth. It is entirely appropriate that in 1865 Jevons should have given to his treatise on the growth prospects of Britain compared with other countries the title *The coal question*. By that date new criteria for deciding the issue were needed. The development of methods whereby the massive reserves of energy locked up in coal deposits could be converted into sources of power and heat for more and more production processes lies very close to the heart of the transition from an advanced organic to a mineral-based energy economy.

The history of the adoption of coal as a key raw material in more and more industries illustrates another aspect of the complexity of the phenomenon referred to as the industrial revolution. It was convenient initially to treat the two modes of economic growth not only as distinct in nature but as successive in time. But foreshadowings of the new system had been of long standing, and especially so in regard to the use of coal. Coal usage did not begin for the first time in the late eighteenth century, or even experience a sudden acceleration in its rate of growth at that time. For several hundred years England had mined far more coal than any other country, and on a steadily expanding scale.[38] A part of her striking relative success during the seventeenth and eighteenth centuries sprang from the special advantages which flowed from the use of coal. In consequence, part of the difficulty in moving from stereotypes of the two systems to a description of the transition between them lies in doing justice to the intermingling of the two in historical reality. This issue will emerge more prominently in the next chapter. Initially it is simpler, and may be less confusing, to limit discussion to stereotypes of the two regimes.

The essential nature of the contrast between them was that between negative and positive feedback systems. An organic economy, however advanced, was subject to negative feedback in the sense that the very process of growth set in train changes that made further growth additionally difficult because of the operation of declining marginal returns in production from the land. It was their appreciation of this point that induced the classical economists to take a pessimistic view of future prospects, especially in relation to real wages.[39] Each step taken made the next a little more painful to take. In parts of an organic economy, because of the effect of specialization of function, increasing returns were obtainable and positive feedback existed, but, since each round of expansion necessarily increased pressure on the land by raising demand for industrial raw materials, as well as food, in the system as a whole negative feedback tended to prevail. In a mineral-based energy economy, in contrast, freed from dependence on the land for raw materials, positive feedback could exist over a large and growing sector of economic

[38] For example, for 1815 Flinn estimates British coal output at 22.6 million metric tons. At that time the output of continental Europe was probably between 3.0 and 3.5 m tons (in 1815 French output was 882,000 tons; in 1817 German output was 1,300,000 tons; Belgian output was probably somewhat greater than French – in 1830 Belgian output was 2,305,000 tons, French 1,760,000 tons; output elsewhere was negligible). Flinn, *British coal industry*, tab. 1.2, p. 26. Mitchell, *European historical statistics*, tab. E2, pp. 381–91.

[39] Adam Smith did not develop the idea of declining marginal returns but further growth became increasingly slow and painful in his 'model', and real wages were more likely to fall than to rise: see Wrigley, 'The classical economists and the industrial revolution', pp. 30–4.

activity. Each step taken made the next easier to take. The system as a whole could gain an increasing momentum of growth. Real wages were not permanently constrained to remain close to the minimum set by the prevailing norms of society.

Further contrasts

Two further contrasts between the organic economy and its successor deserve emphasis. The first relates to agriculture. In organic economies individual farming units had always been ecologically self-contained in the sense that their productive potential was related to, and limited by, factors such as the success of grains and other grasses in capturing the sun's energy and using it in combination with water and other nutrients to provide food for man and fodder for beasts; the quantity of manure per unit area derived from the local farm animals; and the energy made available for cultivation and harvesting by the draught animals supported on locally produced fodder. If energy can be imported from outside the local ecological system in the form of chemical fertilizers, insecticides, herbicides, the mechanical work performed by tractors and other farm machinery, and much capital plant, the levels of output attainable may be transformed. The farm will approximate more and more closely to the factory, its raw material inputs and energy supplies being derived increasingly from the same inorganic sources as secure great changes in productivity outside agriculture. Even in agriculture declining marginal returns no longer apply, or apply only in a radically modified form.

The second change relates to the behaviour of the denominator rather than the numerator in the ratio sum which determines living standards: to reproduction rather than to production. As long as marital fertility is not controlled, and nuptiality and mortality are responsive to economic circumstances, it is not difficult to see the strength of another of the arguments deployed by the classical economists, and used by them to justify a pessimistic view of future prospects. Greater prosperity tends to provoke earlier marriage, reduced celibacy and lower mortality. In consequence population growth rates rise, and in due course the consequent surge in the supply relative to the demand for labour will tend to push wages back towards their former level. This may be well above bare subsistence if high minimum acceptable living standards are supported by appropriate social conventions, but a secular rise in living standards for the mass of the population, though not inconceivable, is a remote possibility.

Two developments may render such pessimism misplaced. The first concerns the absolute rate of economic expansion. Even though it may be true that population growth rates tended to rise in response to enhanced prosperity, it is also true that they were subject to a fairly low upper limit. Before the mortality revolution of the late nineteenth and twentieth centuries expectation of life at birth seldom exceeded forty-five years in large populations. Maximum fertility levels were held down both by the fact that the interval between the successive births of married couples, even when the wife was in her peak years of fertility, was rarely less than two years and often nearer three; and by the conventions of the European marriage system which meant that many women never married, or married late in life.[40] In consequence population growth rates very seldom exceeded 1.5 per cent per annum. If, therefore, economic growth accelerated to, say, 2.0 per cent per annum, the classic Malthusian supposition about the necessary tension between population growth and economic expansion ceased to apply, together with the pessimistic inferences drawn from it.

The second development able to alleviate any problem of over-

[40] At the age-specific marital fertility rates prevailing in England in the whole period between the mid-sixteenth century (when the inception of parish registration first allowed such rates to be calculated) and the end of the eighteenth century, a woman marrying early in life, at twenty years of age, and surviving in marriage throughout the child-bearing period would have had about 7.4 children. In practice, however, the mean age at first marriage was much higher, about twenty-five years, and many women never married, the proportion varying between about 5 and 20 per cent at different periods. These influences reduced average family size substantially (with a mean age of first marriage of twenty-five and 12.5 per cent of women never marrying, the average is reduced to 4.66). Moreover, many marriages were cut short by the early death of one of the spouses. It is not surprising, therefore, that general fertility rates were quite modest. Between the later sixteenth century and the last decades of the eighteenth century the crude birth rate usually lay between 28 and 35 per 1,000. Wrigley and Schofield, 'English population history from family reconstitution', tab. 6, p. 169; and idem, *Population history of England*, tab. 3.1, pp. 528–9.

rapid population growth was the spread of fertility limitation *within* marriage rather than simply *by* marriage, as in the traditional west European system.[41] The adoption of contraception by more and more married couples broke the link between prosperity and a higher growth rate. Indeed, the classic expectation came in time to be reversed. High prosperity coupled with low fertility became the expected relationship by the inter-war period. Once in place this novel feature of the new demographic regime further marginalized many of the arguments once proposed with such confidence by the classical economists.

Conclusion

Such changes, however, were secondary. The central feature of the mineral-based energy economy was its ability to free production from dependence on the productivity of the land; or perhaps the point should be phrased slightly differently. Under this economic system dependence on organic raw materials was much reduced in branches of industry which had been long established, and major new sectors of industry were opened up in which there was little or no consumption of organic materials. Since, simultaneously, the advent of the new system permitted the application of heat and mechanical energy in productive processes on a scale without earlier parallel, the old constraints on the scale of output fell away, unit production costs declined continuously across a wide swathe of industries, and both production and productivity could rise without knocking against the ceiling present in the earlier system. Real income per head, that pivotal if exasperatingly crude measure of economic advance, could, for the first time in human history, rise substantially and progressively in all classes of society. Output could outstrip population; production could distance reproduction. For the first time in human history, poverty, rather than being a necessary feature of the human condition for the bulk of the population,

[41] The immense interest in the west European marriage pattern and its correlates in familial structure and organization have stemmed chiefly from an essay of Hajnal's published in the mid-1960s, 'European marriage patterns'. see also Hajnal, 'Two kinds of pre-industrial household formation systems'; Laslett, 'Characteristics of the western family'; and Smith, 'Fertility, economy and household formation'.

became a matter of social choice. The productive capacity existed to meet all basic human needs with a substantial margin to spare. Whether the capacity was being properly used became an urgent and disruptive social, economic and political issue.

In the later editions of the *Essay on population*, Malthus included a chapter, 'Of the only effectual mode of improving the condition of the poor'. Towards the end of the chapter, he summarized his views in the following terms,

In an endeavour to raise the proportion of the quantity of provisions to the number of consumers in any country, our attention would naturally be first directed to the increasing of the absolute quantity of provisions; but finding that, as fast as we did this, the number of consumers more than kept pace with it, and that with all our exertions we were still as far as ever behind, we should be convinced, that our efforts directed in this way would never succeed. It would be setting the tortoise to catch the hare. Finding, therefore, that from the laws of nature we could not proportion the food to the population, our next attempt should naturally be, to proportion the population to the food. If we can persuade the hare to go to sleep, the tortoise may have some chance of overtaking her.[42]

In the next two chapters I shall describe the features of the economic physiology of the hare and the tortoise that gave them their character in organic economies, and also suggest how the tortoise came to acquire both speed and stamina while the nature of the hare changed equally dramatically as the mineral-based energy economy established itself.

[42] Malthus, *Essay on population* (1826), III, p. 486.

2

The advanced organic economy

Any pre-industrial economy was obliged to accept certain limits to growth set by the fact that the land was almost the sole source not only of food but of the great bulk of the raw materials used in manufacture. Since land was in fixed supply, production could only be expanded by obtaining larger and larger outputs from each existing acre of farmland or by breaking in inferior land, but at some stage it seemed unavoidable that diminishing returns would take hold, making further expansion progressively more difficult and costly. All pre-industrial economies were therefore by definition subject to a form of negative feedback, unable to engender changes capable of securing rising real incomes for the mass of the population. As growth progressed, the obstacles to further growth grew ever more pressing. It was their appreciation of these constraints which led the classical economists to make use of the concept of the stationary state as a device to epitomize the nature of the limits to growth, and to disbelieve in the possibility of a radical and permanent upward movement in real wages.

E pur si muove, – and yet the earth did move; there was a breakout from the confines of the pre-industrial economy. In this chapter I shall try to describe the nature and the extent of the changes taking place in the two centuries preceding the conventional date of the industrial revolution; the kind of growth that was in the mind of Adam Smith when he wrote the *Wealth of nations*; the nature, in short, of an advanced organic economy. But in so doing I shall also point to the developments that later assumed sufficient importance to make it possible to avoid the stationary state.

34

The transformation of agricultural productivity

The single most remarkable feature of the economic history of England between the later sixteenth and the early nineteenth centuries was the rise in output per head in agriculture.[1] Population more than doubled; the number of men engaged in farmwork rose only slightly, and, given that the country remained broadly self-sufficient in food, it follows that output per head must have roughly doubled to levels well above those found elsewhere in Europe.[2] This achievement was the more remarkable in that it came about principally through obtaining larger yields from existing farmland rather than from the breaking in of new land. It is abundantly clear that the average man engaged in agriculture in 1800 was producing far more than his predecessor in 1600 rather than substantially less as might have been expected on the principle of declining marginal returns. In 1800 only four men in every ten in employment were working on the land in England at a time when in other European countries that were broadly self-sufficient in food the comparable figure was probably between six and eight.[3] In Elizabethan times, in contrast, there is no reason to suppose that England was much different from other west European countries. Increased output per head was of great strategic importance in relation to the course of real incomes and, more generally, to structural change in the economy. Put crudely, if six men in ten can devote their energies to secondary or tertiary production and yet be adequately fed, a very different economy will emerge from that which is possible if only two or three men in every ten can be spared from the land without running the risk of mass starvation.

  How was such striking progress secured? The question may be tackled conveniently under two different heads. In the first place, it is clearly important to try to establish how the average man on the

[1] As O'Brien remarked, referring to the period 1660–1820, 'what appears in a European context to be distinctive about British agriculture is not so much its rate of growth as its capacity to augment output while releasing labour for employment in industry and services'. O'Brien, 'Agriculture and the home market', p. 775.
[2] Bairoch estimated that in 1810 the productivity of each male worker in agriculture in England was double that in France or Sweden (measured in millions of calories): Bairoch, 'Niveaux de développement', tab. 1, p. 1096.
[3] See above pp. 12–13.

land in 1800 was able to provide foodstuffs for about 1.5 families in addition to his own whereas his forerunner 200 years earlier had been able to provide only for the needs of his own family and, at most, half those of one other family.[4] Indeed, the extent of the progress to be explained is probably understated when expressed in this way in that the produce of the land also sustained the raw material needs of far larger industries in 1800 than in 1600 and yielded the fodder needed by hundreds of thousands of horses employed in mines, industrial plants and transport. Such demand had risen more swiftly than the demand for food between Elizabethan and Georgian times.

But there is a second question to be considered. In many cultural settings technological changes capable of yielding a major increase in production per head are apt to be dissipated by a rise in the agricultural population equal in scale to the rise in output. If, for example, a higher-yielding strain of rice was introduced in a paddy rice area, or an area adopted double-cropping each year rather than taking only a single crop, the potential gain in output per head might be lost because numbers on the land might rise in step with production. This is the process Geertz had in mind in coining the phrase agricultural involution.[5] It is arguable that the spread of potato cultivation in Ireland, in parts of Scandinavia and in the Alpine lands conforms to the same pattern.[6] At all events it is evident that it is not enough to uncover developments capable of increasing output per head on the land; it is also important to suggest how such potential gains were conserved, rather than being divided, among a rising tide of agricultural families leaving each man no more prosperous than his forefather had been. The English population grew fast but it found employment not on the land but in towns or in non-agricultural

---

[4] The extent of the increase in output and manpower productivity in English agriculture during the seventeenth and eighteenth centuries seems clear. The timing of the changes, however, is increasingly disputed. Economic reasoning casts doubt on the extent of any gain in the later eighteenth century, though empirical evidence remains slight. See esp. Jackson, 'Growth and deceleration in English agriculture'; and Crafts, 'British economic growth, 1700–1831'.

[5] Geertz, *Agricultural involution*.

[6] See Drake, *Population and society in Norway*, pp. 55–74; Connell, *Population of Ireland*, esp. ch. 5; Viazzo, *Upland communities*; also Salaman, *The potato, passim*. Many local studies reveal such a pattern: see, for example, the description in Cole and Wolf, *The hidden frontier*, pp. 151–2.

pursuits in the countryside. Growth in early modern England involved a massive restructuring of the economy rather than a simple enlargement.

Over the years agricultural historians have produced a vast literature about cultivation practices, changing yields, the introduction of new crops, livestock breeding, tenurial arrangements, enclosure, and so on. Comparatively little attention has been devoted either to labour productivity or to the attempt to establish the nature of any contrasts between English and continental conditions and practices.[7] It may be significant, therefore, that one recent study which was exemplary in these respects, that by O'Brien and Keyder, should have lain so much stress on the ratio between pastoral and arable activities as the key factor distinguishing English from French agriculture and enabling much higher levels of labour productivity to be achieved in the former.[8] Differences in the yields of the main cereal crops in the two countries were substantial in the nineteenth century and can be attributed with some confidence largely to the far greater availability of animal manure per cultivated acre in England.[9] It is likely that this advantage was at least as pronounced in the seventeenth and eighteenth centuries. Gregory King's estimates of national livestock at the end of the seventeenth century certainly suggest that this may have been the case.[10]

[7] See, for example, the treatment of labour productivity compared with the treatment of more conventional topics, such as product prices or output per acre, in the volumes of The agrarian history of England and Wales.

[8] O'Brien and Keyder, Economic growth in Britain and France.

[9] 'This contrast between an animal-intensive agriculture in England and a far greater emphasis on arable farming in France is, however, central to the explanation of differences achieved in value added per hectare in the two countries: not only are animal products more valuable, but the density of animals per hectare of arable land was a critical determinant of the level physical yields achieved in the cultivation of grains, vegetables and other crops.' Ibid., p. 115.

[10] The following totals represent a scatter of estimates from well-informed men at various dates from King to the inception of official statistics (totals in millions).

Date	Horses	Cattle	Sheep	Pigs	Area to which estimate refers
c. 1695	1.2	4.9	12.0	3.0	England and Wales
1779	–	3.37	25.6	2.08	England
1812	1.09	3.04	21.78	2.04	Great Britain
1855	1.49	4.40	24.37	2.51	Great Britain
1870	1.27	5.40	28.40	2.17	Great Britain

King's estimates concerning draught animals, however, also suggest a more general point related to labour productivity. In all production processes there tends to be a close connection between the quantity of energy per worker available and the level of output per head attained.[11] Agriculture, by the standards of a pre-industrial economy, was an energy-intensive production process. Soil is heavy and the sod refractory. Getting the hay from an acre of meadow to the barn, or, still more, moving the manure from the farmyard to the field, involves performing a very large number of foot-pounds of effort.

The level of productivity attainable in an agricultural system centring on the hoe and the wheelbarrow is necessarily lower than that which can be reached where the plough takes the place of the hoe, the cart replaces the wheelbarrow and animal muscle is substituted for human muscle. Parallel reasoning suggests that there will also be differences in productivity between agricultural economies where draught animals are numerous and those where they are scarce. The greater the relative importance of pasture compared with arable, the greater the ease with which the ratio of draught animals to human labour can be maintained at a high level. Fodder is just as much a fuel as coal or oil and the energy made available thereby for useful work can transform the output achievable by the individual worker. An increased number of draught animals per 100 men engaged in farmwork, therefore, is likely to mean a higher

---

Notes: King's total for horses in 1695 includes asses. Young's total for cattle in 1779 was probably incomplete (see n. 16); his pig total was derived simply by doubling his total for cows which was a subtotal within his cattle total. The 1812 estimates were for the U.K. They have been adjusted to estimates for G.B. on the assumption that Irish livestock totals were the same proportion of the U.K. total in 1812 as they were in 1855 when McCulloch gives a breakdown between England and Wales, Scotland and Ireland.

Sources: 1695, King, 'Burns Journal', p. 243; 1779, Young, *Political arithmetic*, pt II, p. 28; 1812, 1855, Mulhall, *Dictionary of statistics*, p. 15 (quoting Colquhoun and McCulloch respectively); 1870, Mitchell, *European historical statistics*, tab. D5, p. 326 (these were British official returns).

[11] See, for example, the data showing a relationship between per capita income and energy consumption per annum in Kindleberger, *Economic development*, fig. 4.4, p. 70; or Cipolla, *Economic history of world population*, tab. 4, p. 52.

output per man; or, to put it another way, since animal muscle can be substituted for human muscle in many types of work on the land, human labour can be released from agriculture into other occupations when draught animals are numerous. If, therefore, it were demonstrable that the ratio of draught animals to farmland were higher in England than elsewhere, and especially if the trend in England were upwards in the early modern period, this would be an important element in explaining the divergence in labour productivity trends in agriculture between England and the continent.[12]

A man can produce only about a tenth as many foot-pounds of effort in an hour as a horse, and an abundance of horses or other draught animals can therefore in principle lead to large savings in manpower. Empirical evidence about the interchangeability of the two sources of energy in agriculture in the past is lacking, but a study of Mexican agriculture forty years ago showed fairly close correspondence between theoretical expectation and reality. In maize cultivation a hectare could either be tilled and cultivated by hand, or by using oxen. In the former case, 1,140 man hours of labour were needed; in the latter 380 man hours, plus 200 hours of work by oxen, suggesting that 1 ox hour = 3.8 man hours. An ox is usually taken to produce 0.5–0.75 horse power, which implies that 1 horse hour is equivalent to between 5.1 and 7.6 man hours in this type of agriculture.[13]

Reliable estimates of livestock numbers are not available before the later nineteenth century. Still less is there good evidence about the numbers of horses and oxen used for draught purposes in agriculture. Two points can, however, be made with some confidence.

[12] O'Brien laid emphasis on this point. In reference to the rise in labour productivity, he wrote, 'English farmers produced more food and released labour at the same time. They did so essentially by substituting animals for manpower and fertilizer for land.' O'Brien, 'Agriculture and the home market', p. 779.

The energy output of man is very similar to that of a horse *per unit of caloric intake*, a fact that led Cottrell to remark, 'Where land is plentiful, population sparse, and draught animals available, there may be an economy in substituting draught animals for manpower; but with increased population and competition of land for the production of food and feed, the situation may be reversed, the survival of man being more important than the feeding of work animals.' Cottrell, *Energy and society*, p. viii.

[13] Pimentel, 'Energy flow in the food system', pp. 5–6.

First, Britain enjoyed a substantial advantage over France, and probably over other continental countries in this regard in the early nineteenth century.[14] Second, it is likely that the animal power available for each man engaged in agriculture had been rising significantly in England during the early modern period.

Thompson has recently reviewed the evidence for horse numbers in the nineteenth century and concluded that there was a total of 1.29 million horses in Britain in 1811, of which 0.8 million were farm animals. Both totals rose to an all-time peak in 1901 when they were 3.28 and 1.51 millions respectively.[15] There were still a small number of oxen in agricultural use at the beginning of the nineteenth century but their numbers were probably too few to have represented a significant element in estimating farm animal power.[16] Mulhall quoted an estimate of 19 million acres as the area under crops in the United Kingdom in 1820. Porter gives a very similar figure for a slightly later date (1827), and also divides the total between the four constituent countries of the U.K.[17] Subtracting Ireland suggests a figure for Great Britain of 13.7 million acres. Combining Thompson's estimate for farm horses with the acreage figure, suggests that about 1820 there were 5.8 horses for every 100 arable acres in Britain.

The total number of horses in France is given by Mulhall as 1.84 million in 1812 and 2.5 million in 1830. If we assume a figure of 2.2 million in 1820 and further assume that 55 per cent of all horses were in agricultural use (the comparable figure in 1892 was 47 per cent[18]), the number of such horses was 1.21 million. For

---

[14] The advantage remained throughout the nineteenth century. O'Brien and Keyder, *Economic growth in Britain and France*, tab. 5.5, p. 117.

[15] Thompson, 'Nineteenth-century horse sense', tab. 2, p. 80.

[16] McCulloch, when quoting Arthur Young's 1779 estimate of 3.37 million cattle, suggested that at that date there were in addition 150,000 oxen in England, 'as more oxen were then employed in husbandry than at present': *Statistical account*, I, p. 495.

[17] Mulhall, *Dictionary of statistics*, p. 7. Porter, *Progress of the nation*, p. 160; Porter was quoting from the work of William Couling, a civil engineer and surveyor, reporting to a House of Commons Select Committee.

[18] O'Brien and Keyder quote a total of 1.322 million draught horses in agriculture in 1892, at which date the national horse population was 2.795 million. O'Brien and Keyder, *Economic growth in Britain and France*, tab. 5.5, p. 117; Mitchell, *European historical statistics*, tab. D5, p. 318.

1892 O'Brien and Keyder reported a total of 1.387 million draught cattle in agriculture (the total cattle population was then 13.719 million).[19] Let us assume a figure of 1 million oxen for 1820 (the total cattle population was then c. 6.5 million[20]). Oxen performed less work per hour than horses, worked a shorter day and were considerably less versatile, so that it is reasonable to regard, say, three oxen as equal in work value to two horses.[21] On these assumptions the number of horse equivalents in French agriculture in 1820 was 1.87 millions. The arable area of France was probably about 52 million acres,[22] suggesting a figure of 3.6 horse equivalents for every 100 arable acres in France, or 62 per cent of the comparable British figure. If anything, this estimate probably errs on the high side of the true figure.

Uncertainty about empirical data is even greater in attempting to estimate the extent of any rise in the animal power available for each agricultural worker in England in the early modern period, but the attempt seems worthwhile if only to illustrate the order of magnitude of the gains that may have occurred and their importance in helping to explain the phenomenon of rising rather than declining marginal returns in English agriculture. Gregory King estimated that there was a total of 502,000 'cart and plough' horses in England out of a total of draught horses of all types of 550,200. Arthur Young considered that there were 927,610 'draught cattle' in agriculture in England in 1779, and McCulloch later suggested that of these 150,000 were oxen, leaving an implied total of horses of, say, 775,000.[23] Thompson's figure of 0.8 million farm horses in 1811 refers to Great Britain. It may plausibly be adjusted down to 0.7

[19] Ibid.
[20] Mulhall, *Dictionary of statistics*, p. 20, quotes estimates of 6.08 and 7.13 million for 1812 and 1830.
[21] See, in this connection, Langdon, 'Horses and oxen'; and idem, 'Horse hauling'.
[22] There are statistics for the acreage of the major cereal crops in France and for potatoes from 1815 onwards for most years. In 1820 the combined acreage for such crops was 32.36 million acres; in 1862, 40.28 million acres. For 1859 de Lavergne gives a figure of 64.19 million acres for arable as a whole. On the assumption that cereals and potatoes formed the same proportion of the total arable acreage at both dates, this suggests a figure of about 52 million for the total arable acreage in 1820. Mitchell, *European historical statistics*, tab. D1, pp. 209, 213; Mulhall, *Dictionary of statistics*, p. 19.
[23] King, 'Burns Journal', p. 200; Young, *Political arithmetic*, pt II, p. 31; see also n.16.

million to put it on a comparable basis to King's estimate.[24] The total
number of adult males engaged in agriculture was about 1.0
million in 1811, a total perhaps 10 per cent larger than in Gregory
King's day.[25] Such figures imply a rise of 27 per cent in the horse
power available per man on the land in the course of the eighteenth
century. They also imply, on the assumption that one horse provided
as much energy as five men (it should be borne in mind that horses
normally worked fewer hours per week than men), that horses
provided the equivalent of 2.75 'man power' per adult male in agriculture at the beginning of the eighteenth century and the equivalent of 3.50 'man power' by its end.[26]

Because so much attention has been devoted in the past to output
per acre, the large pastoral element in English agriculture has been
treated as significant because many beasts mean much manure, and
adequate manuring has a dramatic impact on cereal yield. Further,
it has been noted large numbers of farm animals implies a lesser
dependence on corn for food and hence a better balanced diet, and
that a large pastoral sector also reduced the risk of catastrophic
variations in food supply from year to year both because farm
animals are a living food store that can be drawn down in hard times,
and because years that were bad for cereals might be good for grass.
In addition, although the coefficient of variation of *gross* cereal yields
is as large when yields are high as when they are low, the coefficient

[24] In 1855, when the total number of horses in Great Britain was 1.494 million, the
total for Scotland was 0.185 million, or 12.4 per cent of the total. A proportionate
reduction in Thompson's estimate of 0.8 million farm horses yields a total of 0.7
million.

[25] The total number of males aged twenty or more employed in agriculture in
England in 1811 may be estimated at 910,000. In 1831 there were 980,750
males aged twenty or more in agriculture in England, and 95,162 such males in
Wales. If the proportions were similar in 1811, the implied total for England and
Wales is almost exactly 1.0 million. Wrigley, 'Men on the land', tab. 11.12, p. 332;
1831 Census, enumeration abstract, II, *Parliamentary Papers* 1833, xxvii, pp.
924–5.

[26] It is of interest to note that, using the same method of estimation and the horse
power total of 1.87 million already quoted, the comparable figure for an adult male
in French agriculture in 1820 is 2.2 'manpower'. In making this calculation I have
assumed that the total of adult males in French agriculture in 1820 was 4.25
million (in 1856 there were 5.15 million males of all ages in agriculture: Mitchell,
European historical statistics, tab. c1, p. 163).

of variation of *net* yields is substantially reduced when yields are high, thus minimizing the danger of serious fluctuations in food supply where abundant dung has allowed high yields to be obtained.[27] Concentration on these aspects of the characteristic emphasis on pasture in English agriculture, therefore, goes far to explaining how the English population could enjoy a better balanced and stabler food supply than was common abroad. The significance of the extra horse power that could be used to meet the energy needs of agriculture, or indeed of industry and transport, as a result of a high ratio of pasture to arable, has received less attention but may have been of equal or greater importance in fostering economic progress, and especially in raising output per head.

The significance of a relative abundance of energy for farmwork should not be seen solely in terms of the needs of the annual cycle of production, but in relation to long-term improvement of farmland, or, in other words, to capital investment. Arthur Young referred quite casually to the practice of applying marl to farmland at the rate of 100 to 150 tons per acre.[28] Assuming by way of illustration, that 100 acres were marled in this way on a particular farm, and, conservatively, that the marl was brought an average of 2 miles from the marl pit to the field, then treating the 100 acres would involve 30,000 ton-miles of transport, and would require an expenditure of energy implying the use of very large quantities of fodder as fuel, a feat scarcely feasible in the circumstances of peasant agriculture in much of continental Europe. Liberal dressings of marl on suitable soils meant long-term improvement to their productivity; much the same was true of applications of lime, shells, chalk and sand where appropriate, and of the various forms of organic manure.[29] All could effect a significant improvement in yield; all required a comparative abundance of draught animals.

The records of the Buller estates in Cornwall in the mid-eighteenth century provide an insight into the massive importance of activities

[27] This point is explored further in Wrigley, 'Corn yields and prices', p. 113.

[28] Young, *Travels in France*, p. 314.

[29] There is valuable evidence of the scale of such practices in the later seventeenth century, of their relatively recent origin in many areas, and of the recognition of their effectiveness in volume v of *The agrarian history of England and Wales*. For such evidence about Anglesey, for example, see Emery, 'Wales', pp. 395–6.

of this kind in English agriculture at the time. The largest single item in the labour budget of the year was not harvesting, nor ploughing, but sanding, manuring and liming. Of the 7,197 man-days worked in the course of the year on the two estates of Keveral Barton and Morval Barton, 14.0 per cent were devoted to improving the productivity of the soil in this way compared with 12.6 per cent for harvesting and 8.8 per cent for ploughing and preparing the soil.[30] Soil improvement work of this type was heavily concentrated in the late autumn and winter months, thus helping to reduce the seasonal slack in labour use which tended to keep productivity low generally in traditional agriculture. Clearly a substantial fraction of the average English farmer's outlay on wages should be regarded as capital investment in improving the productivity of the farm if the Buller estates were representative of English practice in general.

Though it may be true, however, that there were features of the English agrarian economy conducive to high labour productivity, consolidating the achievement depended on much more than technological change or a favourable pasture to arable ratio. Though one pair of hands might be able to do what had once required two pairs, two pairs might nonetheless participate in the work leaving labour productivity unchanged. Suppose, for example, that the social and familial imperatives determining the decisions of those working the land had been such that no one left the family farm while its produce afforded subsistence to all those present in the household. Then an increase in output would simply have tended to increase the number on the land. More generally, if no one had left the farm until the *average* product of those living on the farm had fallen to the conventional minimum standard of living accepted in the community, rather than the exodus starting when the *marginal* product fell to this level, labour productivity would have been low. In some systems of peasant agriculture, where the social values prevailing underwrote the retention of labour on individual holdings in this fashion, any potential for high labour productivity was apt to be wasted in widespread underemployment.

It is a considerable oversimplification to regard the *dramatis personae* of English agriculture even at the end of the eighteenth

[30] Pounds, 'Barton farming', tab. 4, p. 66, and tab. 10, p. 74.

century as consisting solely of landlords, tenant farmers and landless, wage-paid labourers; but it is fair to identify a trend towards such a caste over the two preceding centuries. And, *pace* Goldsmith, there were, and had long been, few peasants in England, bold or otherwise, with habits of life and mind similar to those still widespread on the continent.[31] A tenant farmer, as Malthus noted in pointing to the merits of capitalist agriculture, could have no reason to keep a labourer on the land unless his product at least sufficed to support himself and his family and to yield an adequate return on the working capital involved. The marginal man must be paid and must earn full subsistence for himself and an average number of dependents.[32] Since productivity at the margin must reach this level, average productivity was necessarily higher. In English agriculture, in short, there was a powerful institutional constraint upon immiseration that might be lacking or less effective elsewhere.

Agricultural and industrial success are closely intertwined in all organic economies. Recall what Adam Smith had to say on this topic:

An inland country naturally fertile and easily cultivated produces a great surplus of provisions beyond what is necessary for maintaining the cultivators, and on account of the expense of land carriage, and the inconveniency of river navigation, it may frequently be difficult to send this surplus abroad. Abundance, therefore, renders provisions cheap, and encourages a great number of workmen to settle in the neighbourhood, who find that their industry can there procure them more of the necessaries and conveniences of life than in other places. They work up the material of manufacture which the land produces, and exchange their finished work, or what is the same thing the price of it, for more materials and provisions. They give a new value to the surplus part of the rude produce, by saving the expense of carrying it to the waterside, or to some distant market; and they furnish the cultivators with something in exchange for it that is either useful or agreeable to them, upon easier terms than they could have obtained it before. The cultivators get a better price for their surplus produce, and can purchase cheaper other conveniences which they have occasion for. They

---

[31] For a powerful statement of the view that typically peasant attitudes were largely absent in early modern, and even medieval, England, see Macfarlane, *Origins of English individualism.*

[32] Malthus, *Essay on population* (1826), III, p. 405.

are thus both encouraged and enabled to increase this surplus produce by a further improvement and better cultivation of the land; and as the fertility of the land had given birth to the manufacture, so the progress of the manufacture reacts upon the land, and increases still further its fertility. The manufacturers first supply the neighbourhood, and afterwards, as their work improves and refines, more distant markets. For though neither the rude produce, nor even the coarse manufacture, could, without the greatest difficulty, support the expense of a considerable land carriage, the refined and improved manufacture easily may. In a small bulk it frequently contains the price of a great quantity of rude produce. A piece of fine cloth, for example, which weighs only eighty pounds, contains in it, the price, not only of eighty pounds weight of wool, but sometimes of several thousand weight of corn, the maintenance of the different working people, and of their immediate employers. The corn, which could with difficulty have been carried abroad in its own shape, is in this manner virtually exported in that of the complete manufacture, and may easily be sent to the remotest corners of the world. In this manner have grown up naturally, and as it were of their own accord, the manufactures of Leeds, Halifax, Sheffield, Birmingham, and Wolverhampton. Such manufactures are the offspring of agriculture.[33]

The process Adam Smith described is an example of the operation of positive feedback. Cheap food and raw materials provided an initial foothold for local manufacture. The development of manufacture, by offering 'conveniences' to local farmers, spurred them on to greater efficiency and larger volumes of production which in turn offered a further stimulus to manufacturing growth, and so on. The congregation of manufacturers at convenient locations turned villages into small towns, and small towns into great cities. The towns that he listed by way of illustration were places highly likely to be included in any list of towns which exemplified the new economic order later to be labelled the industrial revolution, yet, in Adam Smith's eyes, they exemplified the chain of events which could, in favourable circumstances, turn high levels of local agricultural productivity into manufacturing prosperity and generalized economic growth. The vigorous, new urban centres were for him the fruits of an advanced organic economy, not the heralds of a new and different regime.

---

[33] Smith, *Wealth of nations*, ed. Cannan, I, pp. 430–1.

The limits to growth and the standard of living

Adam Smith was adept at identifying elements of positive feedback in the economic system with which he was familiar, but he viewed them as subordinated within a wider economic order which could not hope to achieve a 'take-off' in this way. He did not formulate the principle of declining marginal returns as a fundamental constraint upon economic progress as Malthus and Ricardo were later to do, but analogous considerations led him to a similar conclusion. True, some of the encouraging possibilities he analysed suggested an immense scope for enhanced productivity and therefore, by implication, for improved standards of living. The parable of the pinmakers which he told at the very beginning of the *Wealth of nations* described how the productivity of pinmakers working in a co-ordinated group, each specializing on a particular aspect of the work, and serving a large market, might exceed that of an isolated worker catering for a tiny, local market in the ratio of 240 to 1 or more, while also producing a far more reliable and refined product.[34] The positioning of the parable so early in the work, however, and the frequency with which Adam Smith reverted to the theme of a virtuous circle of connections between better transport, larger markets, greater specialization of function and a cheaper, more uniform and better quality product, has tended to blind some readers of the *Wealth of nations* to the pessimism he expressed about the secular trend of aggregate growth and especially of real income per head.

Adam Smith's reason for pessimism over real incomes, at least for the bulk of the population, the labouring poor, was simple and brutal, resembling the darker forebodings of the early Malthus. He believed that the wives of labourers were very fertile; that in hard times most of their children died young because of the pressures of poverty; that in better times more survived; and that at all times reproductive potential exceeded productive opportunities,[35] so that it was safe to assume that any increase in the demand for labour would rapidly be met by an increased supply, leaving the ratio between the two unchanged, and resulting in an unchanging level of real wages,

[34] Ibid., pp. 8–9.
[35] Ibid., pp. 88–9.

exceeding bare subsistence only insofar as the longstanding conventional minima for an acceptable style of life in the community in question might elevate it above the physiological floor.[36]

In relation to the prospects for growth and general economic progress, Adam Smith's views might be summarized by remarking that he held to a model of growth that was asymptotic in character rather than exponential. Substantial achievement was possible but it was necessarily limited. Opportunities for profitable investment existed but as the more promising ones were taken up, those that remained became steadily less attractive and the rate of return fell. Suggesting that although the current rates of return on investment in different countries were not directly known, they could be inferred from the rates of interest prevailing, he noted that the Dutch government could borrow at 2 per cent, and a man of good credit at 3 per cent, whereas in England a man could not hope to borrow at less than about 4 per cent, and in France and Scotland still higher rates obtained.[37] The prevailing rate of interest was a measure of the closeness with which a country was approaching the stationary state, that state where 'a country . . . had acquired that full complement of riches which the nature of its soil and climate, and its situation with respect to other countries, allowed it to acquire; which could, therefore, advance no further, and which was not going backwards'. In such a state, 'both the wages of labour and the profits of stock would probably be very low'.[38] The lower the rate, the closer to the point where the incentive to invest would prove too weak to persuade entrepreneurs to risk their capital, and the momentum of growth would die away. Holland, for so long the most successful and advanced economy in Europe, was close to the stationary state.[39]

In parallel with his view about the limitations to growth, Adam Smith identified a characteristic investment sequence. He held that

[36] He contrasted, for example, the conventional minima for European populations with those prevailing in China, where, for the Canton boat people, 'Any carrion, the carcase of a dead dog or cat, for example, though half putrid and stinking, is as welcome to them as the most wholesome food to the people of other countries.' Ibid., p. 81, and more generally, pp. 76–90.

[37] Ibid., pp. 100, 102.

[38] Ibid., p. 106.

[39] Ibid., p. 108.

investment in agriculture was always the form of investment which brought with it the greatest benefit to the community, essentially because it enlarged the productive base of the entire system.[40] Everything else was pyramided upon an agricultural base. He also held that investment in agriculture normally offered the highest returns and that this was why investment in the North American colonies had been predominantly of this type. Eventually, however, the best such opportunities would be exhausted and investment in manufacture would assume a more prominent role, to be followed still later by a shift towards investment in commerce, first in the domestic trades, but ultimately in international commerce.[41] Adam Smith believed that Holland had reached this last stage some while ago, and that this accounted both for her earlier dominance of this type of activity and for the increasingly large role played by England in more recent decades as she followed a similar development trajectory.[42]

Later classical economists adopted a similar stance, buttressing the kinds of argument that Adam Smith had used by drawing out the implications of the recently formulated principle of diminishing returns. The most austere and rigorous of Adam Smith's successors, Ricardo, is worth quoting on this range of topics. Having referred to the natural tendency of profits to fall, because more and more labour was needed to secure a unit increase in food output, and having expressed the hope that, 'This tendency, this gravitation as it were of profits'[43] would be checked by advances in agricultural methods, he ended his chapter on profits on a gloomy note.

Whilst the land yields abundantly, wages may temporarily rise, and the producers may consume more than their accustomed proportion, but the stimulus which will thus be given to population, will speedily reduce the labourers to their usual consumption. But when poor lands are taken into cultivation, or when more capital and labour are expended on old land, with a less return of produce, the effect must be permanent. A greater proportion

---

[40] 'The capital employed in agriculture . . . adds a much greater value to the annual produce of the land and labour of the country, to the real wealth and revenue of its inhabitants. Of all the ways in which a capital can be employed, it is by far the most advantageous to the society.' Ibid., p. 385. See also p. 194.

[41] Ibid., bk ii, ch. 5.

[42] Ibid., pp. 395–6.

[43] Ricardo, *Principles of political economy*, p. 120.

of that part of the produce which remains to be divided, after paying rent, between the owners of stock and the labourers, will be apportioned to the latter. Each man may, and probably will, have a less absolute quantity; but as more labourers are employed in proportion to the whole produce retained by the farmer, the value of a greater proportion of the whole produce will be absorbed by wages, and consequently the value of a smaller proportion will be devoted to profits. This will necessarily be rendered permanent by the laws of nature, which have limited the productive powers of the land.[44]

Portents of a new regime

Patently the expectations of the classical economists were falsified by events. Investment opportunities did not gradually dry up; the principle of diminishing returns did not operate with sufficient rigour to prevent exponential growth; whatever the difficulties involved in measuring real incomes effectively there can be no reasonable doubt that all ranks in society have benefitted substantially and progressively in their power to purchase goods and services over the past two centuries. To falsify the expectations of the classical economists required an industrial revolution, the burgeoning of a new economic regime. The character of the new regime will be described more fully in the next chapter, but, in order to understand the striking extent of the success of the English economy in the seventeenth and eighteenth centuries, it is important to pay attention to certain changes which belonged chronologically to the advanced organic period but anticipated in their nature what was to come later.

In describing the early modern England as an example of an advanced organic economy, I have used the adjective 'organic' in quite a different sense from that in which it was used by the early sociologists such as Tönnies when he wrote of the organic solidarity of a *Gemeinschaft*.[45] Similarly, it is helpful to endow the adjective 'capitalist' with a meaning very different from that which it normally carries in economic discussions, a meaning which assists in establishing the nature of a mineral-based economy. All organic economies depended exclusively, or almost exclusively, upon their ability

[44] Ibid., pp. 125–6.
[45] Tönnies, *Community and society*, pp. 33–7.

to capture some part of the flow of energy reaching the earth in the form of insolation, and to preserve a favourable balance between the energy spent in this pursuit and the energy made available by it. Thus in technologically primitive societies, such as hunter/fisher/gatherer groups, the chase, the fishing expedition and the search for edible fruits, nuts, grains and roots had to secure sufficient energy in an edible form to fuel the next round of similar operations. The penalty for any prolonged failure to secure at least as much energy in the form of food as was expended in the search for food was death. Any device which increased the ratio between energy gained and energy expended, as for example the use of a bow rather than a hunting spear, enabled a greater proportion of the waking day to be devoted to activities other than food provision. The development of a method of tapping a larger fraction of the energy flow in the ecological system, as by cultivating grains rather than seeking out scattered individual wild plants, widened the material base of the society and was likely to be adopted provided that the ratio of energy gained to energy expended did not deteriorate as a result. The horse collar and the heavy plough, or the elimination of fallow by suitable crop rotations, are further examples of the constant search for more effective ways of tapping the flow of energy which begins as insolation, is transmuted by photosynthesis into vegetable matter, and then passes on through the food chain into different organic forms.

All such changes, however, have it in common that they are directed at improving the efficiency with which an energy *flow* can be utilized to serve the needs of individuals living together in societies. In advanced organic economies the efficiency of the process may be such that only a minority of the workforce is directly engaged in the production of food and basic raw materials. But all alike must live within limits set by their ability to capture some fraction of a flow whose size varies very little from year to year and not at all in secular trend. They have no access to capital *stocks* of energy which can sharply increase the quantity of energy per head available and so liberate them from the constraints inherent in a fixed flow situation.

The early modern period saw the appearance in England of an important 'capitalist' element in the energy economy. England began to tap energy deposits in the form of coal which had been accumulated over a period of tens of millions of years and represented a stock of energy potential that could be drawn down on a scale that vastly exceeded any energy flow from organic sources that could be tapped by the material technology of the day.[46] In the very long run, of course, a capitalist economy, in this sense of capitalism, must have a finite life. Every ton of coal dug from the pit is a ton less to dig. The quantity of energy which could be drawn from a large coal mine was so immense in relation to contemporary needs, however, that this consideration had relevance only on an extended time scale, and meanwhile the benefits to be drawn from a capitalist economy were very great.

Consider the difficulties inherent in any organic economy in which economic expansion was taking place. The basic needs which had to be satisfied if life were to be sustained, what the classical economists termed the necessaries of life, were, to use Malthus's terminology, food, clothing, lodging and firing.[47] The provision of any one of the four was always in competition with the provision of the other three in that each required the use of land. Tudor governments wrestled with the problem of reconciling the demand for grain with the demand for wool. The same land could not be used for both wheat and sheep. The complaint that sheep were devouring men provided a vivid phrase to spotlight a perennial problem wherever growth was occurring. But the conflicting demands arising from the other two necessaries of life were equally insistent, and have been relatively neglected.

Securing an adequate supply of fuel, for example, was as urgent a problem as securing sufficient food. The importance of fuel is well symbolized in von Thünen's classic analysis of the spatial location of

[46]   The size of the annual flow of energy from the sun is huge but very difficult to capture for human ends. It has been estimated that the annual solar energy receipt of the United Kingdom is 22,640 million tons of coal equivalent (mtce). However, the percentage of solar energy that is fixed by plant tissues is very small. The conversion efficiency of natural vegetation has been variously estimated between 0.1 and 0.4 per cent. At the lower figure, therefore, what can be captured by photosynthesis by natural vegetation is a little over 20 mtce. British coal output passed 20 million tons early early in the nineteenth century. Cultivated plants have higher conversion efficiencies (potatoes 0.4 per cent; wheat 0.2 per cent). White and Plaskett, *Biomass as fuel*, pp. 2, 12; Pimentel, 'Energy flow in the food system', p. 2.

[47]   Malthus, *Principles of political economy*, v, p. 115.

economic activity in an organic economy. Von Thünen, who regarded himself as an intellectual disciple of Adam Smith, and who had practical experience of the running of a large agricultural estate, set himself the task of determining what shape the pattern of land use would assume on a uniform plain at the centre of which there was a market town. Simplifying in this way enabled him to show that transport costs and the rents which various crops could sustain at varying distances from the market would cause concentric bands of land use to appear round the city. The innermost ring would be devoted to market gardening and the production of especially perishable commodities. The second ring, however, would consist of woodland to meet the needs of the town for fuel and building materials, relegating the production of the main foodstuffs to a greater distance. Grain growing and cattle raising, being better able to meet the costs of transportation and still reach the market at an acceptable price, would take place further away from the urban centre.[48]

Modern studies of deeply impoverished rural communities show very vividly how great are the sacrifices which the poor will make in order to secure their minimum fuel needs. A recent study of the village of Ulipur in Bangladesh, one of the poorest of all countries in the world today, revealed that landless agricultural labourers, living on a minimal diet consisting chiefly of husked rice and yielding them each only about 1,600 kilocalories of food a day, if obliged to purchase both food and fuel through the market, would need to spend more than a third as much on the latter as on the former. In the hill areas of Nepal and Pakistan a quarter of total income is commonly spent on fuel.[49] The necessity to spend so much on fuel arises because it takes about three calories of fuel to cook each calorie of food. The better-off peasants enjoy the luxury of cooking by burning crop residues such as rice straw; the landless poor may be obliged to use fuel as unsuitable as the water hyacinth which, when harvested, is 93 per cent water.[50] Fuel was always, of course, needed in far larger quantities in the severer climate of western Europe

[48] Von Thünen, *The isolated state.*
[49] Briscoe, 'Energy use in a Bangladesh village', p. 635.
[50] Ibid., p. 632, and tab. 4, p.630.

where heat is needed to keep dwelling spaces at a tolerable minimum temperature no less than for cooking.

Wood was the prime fuel in western Europe, but England, though once a thickly forested land, had already become more severely deforested than most other neighbouring countries in medieval times. The population recovery of the sixteenth century increased domestic demand for fuel no less than for food or for clothing, with concomitant dangers of a disproportionately rapid rise in fuel costs. The fuel problem in England may never have been as severe as it is in parts of Bangladesh today, but its inhibiting effects should not be underestimated. Industries which required large quantities of heat in their production processes were unable to establish themselves where fuel prices had reached a high level because of household demand alone. Equally, the existence of a source of cheap fuel, and especially of a source able to sustain a very large increase in output without an increase in the unit costs of production, constituted a great opportunity for any industry with large heat needs.

Hence the significance of the new capitalist element in the organic economy of early modern England. Where coal outcropped to the surface and could be mined cheaply, and especially where the outcrops occurred close to navigable water, a great opportunity offered. Throughout the seventeenth and eighteenth centuries coal was dug in Britain on a scale without parallel elsewhere. In 1800 the output of coal in Britain had reached about 15 million tons a year, at a time when the combined production of the whole of continental Europe probably did not exceed 3 million tons. In 1700, when British output was probably between 2.5 and 3 million tons, it has been estimated that it was five times as large as the output of the whole of the rest of the world.[51]

Every ton of coal burned makes available about twice as much heat as the same weight of dry wood, and since an acre of woodland probably did not yield more than about 2 tons of dry wood a year on a sustained basis at the most, it follows that an annual production of, say, 1 million tons of coal provided as much heat as could have been

[51] Unger, 'Energy sources for the Dutch golden age', p. 240. For British output figures, Flinn, *British coal industry*, tab. 1.2, p. 26.

obtained from 1 million acres of forested land.[52] One way of picturing
the effect of the beginnings of a capitalist element in the energy
economy, therefore, is to imagine the cultivable area of the kingdom
being increased by 15 million acres towards the end of George III's
reign, compared with its area when Elizabeth ascended the throne.
The economy benefited from coal use to this extent in that to secure
the same quantity of heat for domestic cooking and heating, glass
manufacture, brewing, dye vats, salt boiling, baking bricks, burning
lime, distilling gin, baking bread, laundry processes, smelting and
working metals, and so on through a virtually endless list of industrial processes, would otherwise have required many millions of
acres to be devoted to growing timber. A fraction only of such needs
could have been met by timber imports. In the absence of a rising
consumption of coal, there would both have been keener pressure on
land, with larger acreages devoted to, say, coppiced woodland and
therefore not available for arable or pasture, and also higher fuel
costs and therefore a less vigorous development of all those
industries which needed heat for production processes.[53] The transition to a partial dependence upon inorganic *stocks* of energy rather
than upon organic energy *flows* played an important role in allowing
the English economy to expand without debilitating pressure on the
land in the early modern period.

Already, therefore, well before the date normally assigned to the
industrial revolution, the dependence of the English economy on
organic raw materials had been significantly reduced, and as a result
constraints upon growth were eased. Of the four necessaries of life
which Malthus had listed one, firing, gradually ceased to entail competition with the other three as the use of coal spread. In the sense in

[52] The heat output of combustion of bone-dry wood is 4,200 kcal/kg compared with
8,000 kcal/kg for bituminous coal. White and Plaskett, *Biomass as fuel*, tab. 1,
p. 12. Forests in northern Europe today yield between 3 and 8 tons of bone-dry
wood per hectare per annum on a sustained yield basis, or 1.2 to 3.2 tons per acre.
Ibid., p. 125.

[53] It is of interest to note that Nef estimated that the quantitiy of timber burnt as fuel
in England about 1700 was equivalent to only about 500,000 tons of coal. Nef,
British coal industry, I, p. 222. He derived his figure from Gregory King's estimate
of the amount spent yearly on timber for firing, and on the assumption that equal
sums spent on wood and coal purchased equal heat value.

which Malthus used the term, that is to supply heat for domestic warmth, cooking and household laundry, the spread was patchy as long as internal communications were so primitive that the price of coal could double within 10 miles of the pithead if taken overland.[54] Universal access to coal for domestic purposes awaited first a canal network and later the railways. But firing for a wide range of industrial purposes was not so restricted since industry could move to locations where fuel was to be had cheaply. Glassworks on the Thames were hundreds of miles from the nearest pit, but entirely dependent for their viability upon access to Tyneside coal at an economic price. Abundance of coal also influenced industrial development in other ways. Adam Smith, for example, noted that, 'all over Great Britain manufacturers have confined themselves to the coal countries'. Interestingly, he did not make this assertion because of the importance of cheap fuel in the production processes but because in countries with cold winters fuel was 'a necessary of life, not only for the purpose of dressing victuals, but for the comfortable subsistence of many different sorts of workmen who work within doors'. Coal was the cheapest fuel and, 'The price of fuel has so important an influence on that of labour, that other areas could not produce as cheaply as on the coalfields because high fuel prices mean high labour costs.'[55]

A second of the four necessaries of life, lodging, was tending towards a similar pattern. Over much of England wood had been the prime construction material both for domestic architecture and for other buildings. The advent of cheap bricks, made possible by the cheapness of heat derived from burning coal, meant a sharp fall in the quantity of the wood needed by the building industry to erect a house, and especially in the large timbers which had once provided the frame round which the house was built. Thus, although a growing population meant a rising demand for firing and lodging it did not mean a proportionate rise in the intensity of competition for vegetable raw materials. The possibility of securing from mineral sources the raw materials required to provide the necessaries of life

---

[54] Flinn remarks that it 'was customarily assumed, in the eighteenth century, that land carriage of coal doubled its pithead price in ten miles'. Flinn, *British coal industry*, p. 146.

[55] Smith, *Wealth of nations*, ed. Cannan, II p. 404.

previously obtained from the limited flow of organic products derived from the soil meant a sensible easing of the pressures which had constantly frustrated prolonged growth in organic economies. Or, to put it in a different way, tapping coal reserves on a steadily increasing scale produced much the same effect as would have resulted from the addition of millions of acres of cultivable land to the landscape of England, making it capable of yielding far more of the fruits of the earth than previously.

The rise and fall of the Dutch Republic

Both the opportunities and the potential pitfalls of a transition to a partial dependence upon a stock of energy resources rather than a flow are well illustrated by the history of the Dutch Republic, which at its apogee in the seventeenth century clearly possessed the most successful economy in Europe. Yet the eighteenth century was a century of stagnation for the Dutch Republic. Alone in western Europe its population failed to increase, and the percentage of the population living in cities fell.[56]

De Zeeuw has recently reviewed the evidence concerning energy use in Holland in the early modern period.[57] His findings have added an interesting new perspective both to the rise and to the decline of the Republic. He noted that the depletion of forest cover created fuel problems in several of the more densely populated areas of western Europe in the sixteenth century, and suggested that, 'Only the Netherlands, of all European countries, came to supplement its soil-dependent energy resources with the large-scale exploitation of its peat stock.'[58] He argued that this did not occur because of the quality of Dutch peat or the scale of peat deposits in Holland but because in no other area were abundant peat deposits situated close to an existing waterway network. By constructing short feeder canals in

[56] The population of the Dutch Republic was already 1.9 million in 1650 and at a very similar level in both 1700 and 1750, rising to 2.1 million by 1800. The proportion of the population living in cities with 10,000 inhabitants or more reached a peak of 34 per cent in 1700, but had fallen to 29 per cent a century later. De Vries, 'Decline and rise of the Dutch economy', tab. 4, p. 172.

[57] De Zeeuw, 'Peat and the Dutch golden age'.

[58] Ibid., p. 5.

the peat fields all the major urban areas gained access to a supply of peat at a low price. The scale of peat consumption in the seventeenth century can be estimated approximately. It appears from de Zeeuw's estimates that peat alone was providing as large an annual quantity of energy for the Dutch economy in the seventeenth century as the total national energy consumption about 1840 when for the first time approximate energy consumption statistics were collected. By then, however, the population was 50 per cent larger, so that energy consumption per head had fallen considerably (and about two-fifths of the energy use came from imported coal).[59]

De Zeeuw suggested that the availability of very cheap fuel in great abundance explains the success of heat-intensive industries in the Dutch golden age: brewing, brick and tile manufacture, salt refining, distilling, bleaching, dyeing and printing textiles, madder and chicory works, drying houses, and so on. He attributed the outstanding success of Dutch industry and commerce to the competitive advantages afforded by cheap energy; the relatively high wages paid in Holland to this success; and the tendency to favour capital-intensive investment to the high price of labour.

Whether or not these inferences are acceptable, it seems clear that this form of capitalist exploitation was foredoomed to a brief existence. At a conservative estimate between 3 and 5 per cent of the entire reserve of workable peat was extracted on average in each decade during the seventeenth century.[60] Physical exhaustion and rising marginal costs were unavoidable over a relatively brief span of time. A seventeenth-century Dutch Jevons, contemplating his country's future in the same way that the nineteenth-century Englishman did when he wrote *The coal question*, would have been drawn to an even more pessimistic view than Jevons came to in assessing the future of an industrial country that had become heavily depen-

---

[59] Ibid., p. 14–16,

[60] De Zeeuw estimates the entire volume of workable peat originally available in Holland as $6.2 \times 10^9 \text{m}^3$, and suggests a figure of $15.5 \times 10^6 \text{m}^3$ per annum as the rate of extraction of peat during the seventeenth century. Allowing for the fact that a substantial quantity had been dug before 1600, and that some reserves were economically inaccessible before the transport improvements of the nineteenth century, a rate of effective depletion of 3 to 5 per cent per decade is perhaps a conservative estimate. Ibid., pp. 6–14, esp. tab. I, p. 9 and tab. II, p. 14.

dent on coal, and therefore vulnerable to any lack of comparative advantage in the scale, distribution and accessibility of coal reserves.

De Zeeuw estimated that in the seventeenth century Holland was producing a little more than 1.5 million metric tons of peat a year.[61] A ton of peat produces only the same heat as about half a ton of coal, and therefore English mines in 1700 were producing between 3 and 3.5 times the heat equivalent of Dutch peat beds, since the annual production of coal about that date was roughly 2.5 million tons.[62] On a per caput basis, and in heat equivalent terms, English coal production matched or slightly exceeded Dutch peat extraction by the end of the seventeenth century, [63] but the capital basis of English coal production was far stronger, since the coal measures under English soil could sustain far higher levels of output than were reached in the seventeenth and eighteenth centuries for hundreds of years, even millennia, provided that a solution could be found to the pressing difficulties of pit drainage and coal winding as the seams nearest to the surface were exhausted.

It may well be that de Zeeuw's estimates overstate the scale of Dutch energy production in the seventeenth century. His assertions about the dominance of peat in supplying Dutch energy needs have been called in question recently by Unger.[64] Unger suggested that de Zeeuw overestimated the quantity of peat extracted each year, and the calorific content of peat per unit weight, but underestimated the normal extent of shrinkage between extraction and use (which would affect his calculation of its energy potential since the latter was based on a measure of volume). Unger's preferred estimate of the annual consumption of thermal energy derived from peat is only a fifth as large as de Zeeuw's.[65] Unger also emphasized the significant

[61] Ibid., tab. III, p. 16.

[62] Flinn, *British coal industry*, tab. 1.2, p. 26, estimates the total output of all British coalfields in 1700 as 2.985 million tons, of which 0.45 m tons was produced in Scotland, and 0.105 m tons in Wales.

[63] The population of England in 1700 was just over 5 million while the Dutch population was about 1.9 million, so that the ratio of population sizes in the two countries was a little smaller than the ratio of energy consumption. Wrigley and Schofield, *Population history of England*, tab. A3.3, pp. 531–5; de Vries, 'Decline and rise of the Dutch economy', tab. 4, p. 172.

[64] Unger, 'Energy sources for the Dutch golden age'.

[65] Ibid., pp. 226–7.

part played by imported coal in meeting Dutch energy needs as peat supply problems multiplied in the eighteenth century. As he stressed, however, his revisions leave de Zeeuw's main argument largely untouched.[66] Even on his much lower estimates of the energy production from peat, it was by far the most important source of heat energy in the seventeenth century, and the absolute quantity of heat produced in this fashion was very substantial. Although Holland was able to supplement her peat supplies with coal imports from England (and also, to a lesser extent, from the Liège area) large-scale switching was hindered by English export duties, Dutch provincial import duties and by the costs of break-of-bulk trans-shipment at Dutch ports which left Dutch industries at an increasing disadvantage in competition with their English rivals.[67] Neither the splendid high noon of Dutch wealth and power in the seventeenth century, nor the darkening horizon of the later eighteenth century, can be explained solely in terms of fuel resources and costs but the Dutch experience affords a most instructive contrast with what happened in England.

Conclusion: prices and welfare in an advanced organic economy

In spite of the substantial and growing importance of a mineral-based, 'capitalist' element in the English economy of the early modern period it seems appropriate to describe it as an advanced organic economy and to contrast it with what was to succeed it in the course of the nineteenth century. Though land was relieved of some of the pressures to which it would otherwise have been subjected because firing and lodging needs were increasingly met from outside agriculture, the advances made by agriculture were striking. A doubling in both output per acre and output per head even over as long a period as two centuries was a notable achievement in a country already long settled, and agriculture remained by far the largest industry. Its performance largely determined that of the economy as a whole.

---

[66]   At least as far as the seventeenth century is concerned. Even on Unger's revised figures, peat remains the dominant energy source until well into the eighteenth century. Ibid., pp. 225, 246.

[67]   Ibid., pp. 234–5, 243–4.

There are, moreover, other reasons to emphasize continuity with the past. In particular, if the level and trend of real incomes is the prime touchstone of economic progress, the defining characteristic of an industrial revolution, then the seventeenth and eighteenth centuries appear to have had more in common with earlier than with later centuries. Malthus displayed a great interest in the question of long-term trends in real wages. In the *Principles of political economy* he devoted two substantial sections of the chapter 'Of the wages of labour' to empirical evidence about the course of corn wages since the reign of Edward III and the conclusions to be drawn from this survey. His findings resemble closely those of Phelps Brown and Hopkins published in the 1950s.[68] The later fifteenth century emerges as a golden age for the labourer in both exercises. His daily wage, according to Malthus, would at that time have purchased 2 pecks of wheat, whereas in the mid-seventeenth century, close to the nadir of this measure of well-being, the comparable figure was only 7/12 of a peck, rising thereafter to 1 peck in the mid-eighteenth century, only to fall to 5/6 of a peck about the turn of the century, and to rise once more to just over 1 peck after the end of the Napoleonic wars when grain prices fell faster than money wages.[69]

Malthus's discussion of the evidence he had garnered was cautious and sophisticated. He was aware, for example, of the possible effects of the depreciation of the currency following the arrival of New World silver in depressing real wages in the Elizabethan period; he understood the significance of unemployment and underemployment in affecting actual earnings; and he stressed that for most purposes it was the level of family earnings rather than the wages of adult males in employment that determined living standards.[70] Moreover, in common with the other classical economists, he recognized that, although corn wages in England in, say, 1800 were no higher than they had often been during the past half millennium, and were substantially lower than in the fifteenth century, it did not follow that the standard of living generally had shown no improvement.

[68] Phelps Brown and Hopkins, 'The prices of consumables, compared with builders' wage-rates'.

[69] Malthus, *Principles of political economy*, v, pp. 195–204.

[70] Ibid., pp. 188–9, 199–200.

The principal reason for this apparent paradox was that the other necessaries of life were cheaper in terms of wheat than in the past. The cotton industry in the later eighteenth and early nineteenth centuries provided the classic instance of rapidly falling unit costs of production, which implied that whatever money the average family might have to spend on non-food items would secure many more yards of cotton cloth than in the past. But the cotton industry was not alone in this respect. Wherever Adam Smith's parable of the pinmakers epitomized recent change, the same point held true. Other changes might have similar effects, as when coal supplanted wood for firing, or brick replaced wood in construction.

Yet basic rhythms of great importance remained little changed, and the view taken by the classical economists that, save for relatively brief interludes when bursts of prosperity might temporarily take production clear of population growth, gains in production would be matched by a proportionate rise in numbers seems largely justified in relation to the advanced organic period. The varying pace of population growth in England from mid-Tudor times onwards is now known fairly accurately. When compared with the behaviour of a price index dominated by food prices it suggests very strongly that the age-old constraints of organic economies remained powerful. Periods of rising population growth rates were associated with rising food prices; when population was falling, the prices of agricultural products fell; when one measure was stationary, so was the other.

The closeness and consistency of the relationship between the two variables is shown in figure 2.1. In order to minimize the otherwise powerful effect on prices of adventitious harvest fluctuations, the changes in prices were derived from a twenty-five year moving average of the price index. The dates given show the behaviour of the variables over the preceding quarter-century. Thus, for example, the peak rate of growth in prices occurred over the period from 1781 to 1806 when prices were rising at about 2.2 per cent per annum in the series representing a twenty-five year moving average of the basket of consumables index calculated by Phelps Brown and Hopkins. Over the same period population was rising by about 1.1 per cent per annum. The two broad, broken lines indicate that over a period of two-and-a-half centuries changes in the growth rates of population

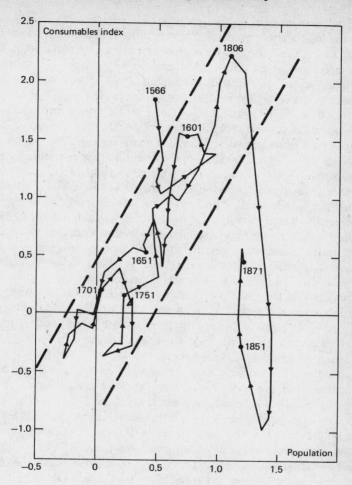

Figure 2.1
Percentage annual rates of growth of population and of a basket of consumables index
Note: for details see accompanying text.
Source: Wrigley and Schofield, *Population history of England*, fig. 10.2, p. 405.

and prices were remarkably closely linked, with the lines representing the belt of readings passing through the origin of the graph. It would be difficult to imagine a more convincing demonstration of the directness of the connection between population growth and pressure upon agricultural production. Only in the nineteenth century was the old link broken. Population growth accelerated still further early in the nineteenth century but food price increases fell sharply to fluctuate round the line representing zero change.

It is true that population grew far more vigorously in England between 1550 and 1800 than in continental Europe, and, so far as real income data are to be trusted, without causing a secular decline in living standards. Indeed, it is striking that the belt of points in figure 2.1 forms a straight line, not a curved one. It might have been expected that high population growth rates would have resulted in a disproportionately rapid rise in prices. English agriculture proved strikingly successful in meeting the challenge of rapid increase in demand. It is also true that living standards were at a relatively high level and that England was free from some of the more grievous afflictions of organic societies, notably the heavy loss of life following serious harvest failure, but the secular tendency of population to advance *pari passu* with the growth of the economy is clear, even though there were lengthy periods when either population growth outstripped production or vice versa.

Figure 2.2 shows the relation between population growth and real wages. It uses the same conventions as the previous figure. Real wage data, like the price data, were taken from a twenty-five year moving average. Although the tightness of relationship is a little less pronounced than in the case of prices, the figure shows a strong connection between an increasing rate of population growth and a decline in real wages. As may be seen from the broad path traced out by the individual points in figure 2.2, in the period of the advanced organic economy England was able to sustain a rate of population growth of about 0.5 per cent per annum while also maintaining real wages. At lower levels of population growth real wages rose, but at any rate significantly above 0.5 per cent per annum the living standards of the labouring poor were clearly under serious threat, and the pattern in the later eighteenth century was not greatly dif-

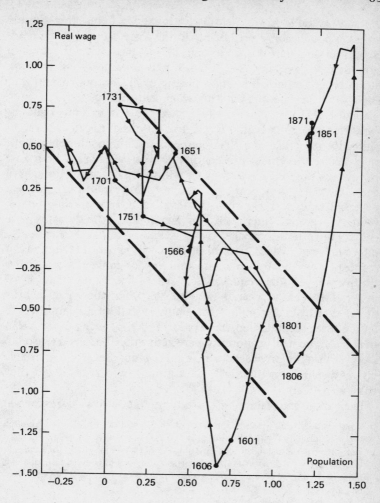

Figure 2.2
Percentage annual rates of growth of population and of a real wage index
Note: for details see accompanying text.
Source: Wrigley and Schofield, *Population history of England*, fig. 10.4,
p. 410.

ferent from that 200 years earlier during the last preceding marked surge in population growth. Only in the early decades of the nineteenth century were the traditional shackles càst off. The population growth rate remained very high, but real wages were growing steadily rather than plunging catastrophically, as might have been expected from the experience of earlier centuries.

English real wage data for this period suffer from many deficiencies,[71] but it is unlikely that they are so serious as to call in question either the existence of a close connection with population growth rates before the nineteenth century or of a clean break with past patterns as the nineteenth century wore on. The closing decades of the advanced organic economy were not a favourable period for real wages. There was no smooth advance as the momentum of economic growth increased. As population growth rates rose sharply towards the peak level reached about 1815, the evidence for improving real wages, so firm in the early part of the eighteenth century, fades away. It remains a matter for controversy whether the overall, national trend was up, down or flat between, say, 1770 and 1820, even between 1750 and 1840, but there can be little doubt that over the bulk of the southern half of England, where agriculture predominated, times grew harder.[72] During the period in which the classical economists were active they had good reason to view long-term prospects with concern despite the remarkable vigour displayed by industries like cotton, of which, of course, they were well aware.[73]

Even at the end of the eighteenth century, Malthus's hare was still

[71] They relate to adult males in employment; they tend to be drawn from a limited range of occupations; and they are heavily biased regionally. They are therefore a very uncertain guide to the standard of living of individuals living in families in which there were often several wage earners, only one of whom was usually an adult male, and all of whom were exposed to periodic unemployment or underemployment.

[72] In this respect the Phelps Brown and Hopkins index, which was based on southern rural wage data in the main, is probably a tolerably reliable guide. It suggests a substantial fall in real wages for two or three generations after a peak in the 1730s. The PBH data reworked to eliminate gaps may be found in Wrigley and Schofield, *Population history of England*, app. 9, pp. 638–44.

[73] See, for example, Malthus, *Essay on population* (1826), III, p. 395; and idem, 'On political economy', pp. 281–2.

displaying an alarming tendency to outpace his tortoise. He and his contemporaries feared for the future. Limits to economic growth seemed near and pressing; constraints on population growth, other than the brutal necessities imposed by the need for food, might prove too feeble to prevent increasing misery. In the event their worst fears were not realized; indeed their best hopes were exceeded. For this to occur implied a striking change from the accustomed pattern of relationships governing the scale and type of material production, and also from those linking production and reproduction. The advanced organic economy in England had already departed substantially from its 'pure' form. In the course of the nineteenth century it was to be replaced by a new economic mode, and a new demographic order also began to take shape. Not only were the powers of locomotion of the tortoise transformed; an unwanted somnolence began slowly to steal over the hare.

3

The mineral-based energy economy

The strident note of indignation about the condition of the working classes so audible in the writing of Karl Marx reflected a real change in economic circumstances over the preceding half-century. It was not that the lot of the average wage earner had deteriorated in recent decades; it may well have improved. It was rather that by the 1860s it was plain that the productive capacity of society had grown greatly and could be expected to rise much further; the era of exponential growth had dawned but it was uncertain whether all members of society, or only a restricted class of people, would benefit from the change. When Malthus had engaged in his prolonged controversy with Godwin two generations earlier he had been able to argue with conviction that while Godwin might hypothesize that general economic well-being and adequate leisure for recreation were attainable goals, both empirical evidence and theoretical considerations suggested that a life of physical toil and intermittent hardship was almost inevitable.[1] In Marx's day the capacity to produce was visibly growing by leaps and bounds and it no longer seemed utopian to suppose that human toil could be abbreviated and yet production

[1] Malthus took strong exception to Godwin's trust in the capacity of the human mind to overcome present problems, preferring to rely on past experience. 'I expect that great discoveries are yet to take place in all the branches of human science, particularly in physics; but the moment we leave past experience as the foundation of our conjectures concerning the future; and still more, if our conjectures absolutely contradict past experience, we are thrown upon a wide field of uncertainty, and any one supposition is then just as good as another.' Malthus, *Essay on population* (1798), p. 83.

might be expanded to match human need. Sometime during the first two-thirds of the nineteenth century Malthus's tortoise acquired an unprecedented speed and stamina.

The arithmetic requirements for a substantial and sustained rise in real income per head were straightforward. Before the revolutionary changes in public health and medicine which started in the later nineteenth century, the highest attainable rate of growth of population was only about 1.5 per cent per annum, or 2.0 per cent on the most extreme assumptions. The tension between population and production would therefore be relaxed if the rate of growth in output could be raised to about 1.5 per cent per annum or higher. The volume of output would rise faster than the number of consumers, and real incomes could rise even if the population growth rate was at or near its maximum. If for any reason rates of population growth stayed below their maximum the potential gain in real incomes would be larger and faster. During the nineteenth century economic growth rates rose to levels far higher than had ever been consistently attained previously while demographic growth rates held roughly steady for most of the century before beginning their secular decline towards its end. By 1900 it was becoming clear that while the earnings of the working classes relative to the richer groups in society had improved little if at all, their absolute standard of living had risen roughly in step with other groups. The cake was growing faster than the numbers round the table and all those present at the meal were benefiting from its greater size.

The classical economists had anticipated that growth must become increasingly difficult and must end in the supervention of the stationary state. In seeking to understand the onset of sustained economic growth at a higher annual rate, the occurrence of an industrial revolution, we may begin by examining the reasons why their expectations were not fulfilled. The central issue in their view had been the question which crystallized as the principle of declining marginal returns in the writings of the later members of the school. If increasing outlays of labour and capital proved necessary in order to win unit increases in food output, real wages would start to fall and the proportion of total expenditure devoted to food would rise, thus cutting the ground from under any tendency towards growth in industrial production. In time, of course, the situation would stabilize since worsening conditions for the labouring poor would prevent further growth in numbers or even precipitate a fall, but meanwhile all momentum of general economic growth would be lost.

The logic of the principle of declining marginal returns in agriculture is impeccable. It can only fail to be exemplified if the assumptions which it embodies are unjustified. Several different developments combined first to postpone and later to cancel its operation in nineteenth-century England.

First, as the classical economists themselves had stressed, technical or organizational advance might permit increases in agricultural output to be obtained from constant or declining inputs of labour and capital for each unit increase in output secured. Better crop rotations; new types of food plant; more effective drainage methods; changes in technique such as the substitution of the scythe for the sickle, or the introduction of sowing machines; the consolidation of farming units; better selection of breeding stock and seed; cheaper and more effective methods of storing, processing and distributing agricultural products; all these and many other comparable changes could postpone the evil day and were in evidence in English agriculture.

Second, improved transport facilities were important both in encouraging regional specialization among domestic farming regions and in enabling food imports to take place on an increasing scale. Since the world contained much unsettled land of high potential and also large tracts long settled but underexploited for lack of a suitable market, there was much scope here too for evading for many decades, perhaps even for centuries, the apparently inevitable tightening of supplies.

Third, there was a continued alleviation of pressure on the land as it became more and more exclusively a purveyor of food alone and no longer the prime source of almost all raw materials of use to man. The changes already in train during the advanced organic period became more pronounced. Coal rather than wood came to supply almost all fuel needs. Where inland transport had once depended upon the cart horse, the carriage horse, the pack horse and the barge horse, it came to depend rather upon the railway engine and in due course the motor lorry. The building industry similarly based itself

more and more heavily upon mineral raw materials. As the traditional competing demand for fertile land to secure supplies of the four
necessaries of life became less severe, agricultural acres could be
devoted more exclusively to food production; the demand for
lodging, firing and even, eventually, for clothing was met from other
sources. The vastly enlarged energy needs of the economy for
general industrial purposes, which would once have been met from
organic sources, were now almost exclusively supplied by the coal
industry.

The energy balance in agriculture

None of these changes would finally have banished the spectre
which haunted the classical economists as they contemplated the
future. All alleviated the problem significantly but rising food costs
might still ultimately have inhibited further growth but for a further
change of an even more fundamental nature. Farms had always
previously been ecologically self-contained units in one important
sense, even though producing for market and often meeting a substantial part of their own food needs via the market. By suppressing
the original vegetation and substituting plants of his choice, the
farmer sought to maximize the quantity of food available for himself,
for his customers and for his farm animals. But he was limited by the
degree of the success of his domesticated plants in trapping the flow
of energy from the sun by photosynthesis. Some of the energy thus
trapped was used directly as human food, some indirectly after being
fed to animals subsequently slaughtered for human consumption,
and some was converted into mechanical energy either by human or
by animal muscle to enable farming operations to be carried out. But
no farmer could continue unless he kept a favourable balance
between the quantity of energy derived from farming operations and
the quantity expended in carrying them out. This ratio in
organic economies was commonly of the order of 10:1 or higher. No
energy was imported from outside the farm, or at least from outside
the farming sector.

From very small beginnings in the first half of the nineteenth
century this condition was slowly relaxed in English agriculture
until today the input of energy into the farming sector vastly exceeds
the energy output from it in the ratio of about 3 to 1.[2] Chemical

---

[2] Grigg, *Dynamics of agricultural change*, p. 80.

fertilizers and pesticides represent one type of external energy input. Another occurs in the obvious form of a vast range of agricultural machines from tractors and combine harvesters to milking machines and grain driers, all of which contribute to raising agricultural output and productivity but use external energy sources. Farms have become specialized, open-air factories whose levels of production can be increased spectacularly provided that large quantities of energy derived from outside the farm can be transmuted on the farm into an increased flow of agricultural products. Modern industrial economies, so far from being afflicted by the problems of declining marginal returns and shortages of food, are embarrassed by agricultural overproduction.

In the main this has been a development of the twentieth century but its beginnings may be found in the nineteenth century. The use of tile drainage, for example, was an early, if minor, illustration of the new trend since it represented an import of energy from outside the farm sector. Steam engines used for threshing were a further instance of the application to a farming operation of a source of mechanical energy not produced on the farm. Eventually hundreds of thousands of farm horses were rendered obsolete by the tractor and the lorry, a change which released a vast acreage from growing fodder as fuel for horses and allowed the land to be used instead for human food production.[3] So enormous was the growth in labour productivity in agriculture in the wake of these changes that one fiftieth of the labour force can provide for the food needs of the whole population today whereas in organic economies the comparable fraction was commonly four-fifths, and it was evidence of the singular achievements of English agriculture in the early modern period that by 1800 only two-fifths of the adult male labour force worked in agriculture.[4]

The changes that took place in agriculture removed a constraint

---

[3] McCulloch, for example, considered that there were about 1.5 million horses in Britain and that 5 acres were needed for the maintenance of each horse. *Statistical account*, I, pp. 489–90. He added, 'If 60 acres, therefore, should be assumed as the average extent of land that may be kept in cultivation by 2 horses, the produce of 10 acres of this will be required for their maintenance' (p. 490).

[4] In 1986 the total employment in agriculture, forestry and fishing was 319,000, or 1.5 per cent of the national employment total of 21,548,000 (male employment was 11,879,000). Central Statistical Office, *Monthly digest of statistics*, no. 496, April 1987 (London, H.M.S.O., 1987). For male employment in agriculture in 1800, see Wrigley, 'Men on the land'.

that had prohibited rapid and sustained growth in the past. But the essential change lay elsewhere. Always previously a productive agriculture had been the base of the whole span of economic activity because all industrial processes depended principally or exclusively on organic raw materials. The new age was built upon different foundations. The fruits of the earth were increasingly used as food alone. It was not from the soil but from beneath the soil that the raw materials of a new economic age were drawn. On the basis of mineral wealth it proved possible to construct an industrial society with a capacity to produce material goods of use to man on a scale that dwarfed such production in any earlier period.

The energy revolution in manufacturing industry

The issue that deserves to be considered first in contemplating the new age is the question of energy availability and usage. In the writings of the classical economists the principal explanation of the attainment of increased output per man lay in the conjunction of a larger accessible market, improved transportation and a greater specialization of function. The mutual interaction between the three could facilitate very large increases in manpower productivity. Adam Smith used the case of the pinmakers to demonstrate the scale of the possible improvement; John Stuart Mill preferred to use the example of the manufacture of playing cards, borrowed from Say, as an illustration of the same theme.[5] Almost any type of handicraft manufacture, however, would lend itself in some degree to the same argument, and all the classical economists regarded specialization as the prime vehicle of economic advance.

Though the scale of possible advances in productivity in this mode may be very substantial, however, they are also finite, perhaps a subsidiary reason why the classical economists looked to a future stationary state. A metal worker living in a village of a hundred families who occasionally turns his hand to pinmaking may make very few pins in a day, and those crude and brittle. If the market broadens to comprise a county of 100,000 people and, say, twenty workmen collaborate to develop the specialisms listed by Adam Smith, they may be able to meet the needs of the whole county and deliver much better and cheaper pins to every housewife, tailor and dressmaker. If, however, the market were to broaden still further to

[5] Mill, *Principles of political economy*, I, p. 123.

consist of 1,000,000 people it is probable that any further gains in output per head would be very slight since the process had already been broken down into its basic elements and further subdivision of function would have ceased at the smaller market size.

As it happens the energy expended by pinmakers on each of the separate operations of pin manufacture is slight, and the chief limitation on further gains in output per head when the market has grown to the size at which functions are fully subdivided is the speed of movement of the pinmaker's hand; but in a large number of industrial processes the energy expended by the worker is considerable and his physical strength is a main limitation upon the level of productivity he can achieve. Many tools and machines are, indeed, inoperable unless the strength in a human arm is supplemented by another power source. A man can wield a hoe but cannot pull a plough; he may be able to pound a pestle within a mortar but he cannot turn a grindstone. The English economy had long been comparatively rich in sources of mechanical power, an indirect benefit of a productive agriculture. Draught animals were of great importance in mining, transport, building and manufacturing industry. Horse gins kept the coal mines free from water as the shafts sank deeper. Several of the key advances in textile machinery in the eighteenth century were initially designed with horse power in mind as a power source, and horses were an important source of such energy until the last decades of the century and beyond.[6]

[6] See, for example, the scattered references to horse-driven machinery in the cotton and woollen industries in the eighteenth century in Musson, *British industry*, pp. 78–90; also Hills, *Power in the industrial revolution*, pp. 88–92: Hills notes that in 1791 in Oldham parish most of the mills were horse-driven because 'the best water sites had been taken' (p. 91). Von Tunzelmann remarks that Hargreaves's jenny and Crompton's mule were developed for animal-powered mills; that Cartwright's mill at Doncaster incorporated power-looms driven by oxen; that Paul and Wyatt used asses to power their roller spinning frames; and that Arkwright initially used horses for his improved frame: *Steam power and British industrialization*, pp. 117–18. As an instance both of the importance and of the unhandiness of animal power in the building industry, see the illustration of the six-horse 'crane' in use to hoist large girders during the construction of the Crystal Palace for the 1851 Exhibition. Ubbelohde, *Man and energy*, p. 43.

It may be noted that it has been estimated that in the United States in 1850, work animals, principally horses, produced 53 per cent of the work from all sources of energy, compared with 13 per cent from manpower, 9 per cent from water power, 6 per cent from wood and 6 per cent from coal: Cook, *Man, energy and society*, p. 63.

Because energy availability exercises such a powerful influence on productivity per head, the development of another source of mechanical power using inanimate energy to supplement human and animal muscle afforded a second main vehicle to secure increased output per head in almost all types of primary and secondary industry. A steam hammer can accomplish feats beyond the stoutest blacksmith. Moreover, since, using inanimate sources of energy, the power available per worker could be increased at need, this mode of increased productivity was intrinsically less closely bounded than the other mode via specialization. Specialization growth might be likened to change by the inheritance of acquired characteristics, consisting of a closely linked set of marginal improvements; power growth to change by mutation, in its suddenness, its unpredictability and its scale.

Power availability per worker, however, did not attract the extensive and systematic treatment by the classical economists that functional specialization received. Given the assumptions which governed their appreciation of growth possibilities, this is not surprising. For most industrial and agricultural processes human muscle could be supplemented only by animal muscle, and, great though the value of such assistance was, it was necessarily limited and generated the same competing pressures for access to a scarce resource common to all animate life in an organic economy. Other sources of mechanical power, principally the windmill and the water wheel, though not subject to the same problems, were not capable of transforming the overall power situation. Wind energy was intermittent and apt to be most abundant on sites that were least convenient in other respects. Water power was also subject to seasonal variations and interruption according to the vagaries of precipitation and the effects of freezing weather, and was subject to rising marginal cost of provision since the better sites were naturally developed first, leaving smaller or less conveniently situated falls for later exploitation. Quite apart from these disadvantages, and notwithstanding their great value for particular applications, neither wind nor water power was available on a scale sufficient to hold out any hope of radically transforming the prospects for output per head and hence of living standards.

Yet such a transformation was a *sine qua non* of the kind of changes in productivity that could qualify as an industrial revolution. Production became concentrated in single buildings or building complexes not to facilitate specialization of function, nor to simplify supervision, except to a minor degree, but to allow mechanical power to be applied to production processes on a larger scale and so to magnify many times over the quantity of work that was performed by each worker. Sometimes the machines in the factories built round a steam engine as the prime mover were in essence closely similar to those previously driven by muscle but they could be made to operate faster and longer than would have been possible in a craft workshop, and, above all, one man might have oversight of, say, half a dozen machines simultaneously where, without the assistance of an inanimate power source, he must have confined himself to a single machine for which he himself provided the mechanical energy.

In transport improvement, the midwife of increasing market size and greater specialization, it was the same story. The railway indeed became the most evocative single image of the new age. New power sources radically reduced costs and increased capacity. In both transport and industry productivity could be increased virtually without limit if the power per worker were raised commensurately. The French economist and demographer Emile Levasseur, writing in the 1880s, expressed the nature of the change in a vivid metaphor. Reviewing the huge increase in the use of steam power in the French economy in the previous forty years, he noted that, if one steam horse power was taken as the equivalent of twenty-one men, in 1840 French industry and commerce had at its disposal the equivalent of just over 1 million labourers in this new form. These were, as he put it, 'true slaves, the most sober, docile and tireless that could be imagined'. By 1885–7 the number had grown to 98 million, 'deux esclaves et demi par habitant de la France', 2.5 slaves for each inhabitant of France.[7] Englishmen, of course, were slave owners on a much larger scale.[8]

Hard-working mechanical slaves had large appetites. They fed on

[7] Levasseur, *La Population française*, III, p. 74.
[8] In 1850, for example, the capacity of French steam engines was about 46 per cent of those in Britain; in 1880 about 40 per cent; and in 1896 43 per cent. Landes, 'Technological change', tab. 48, p. 449. In per caput terms the relative percentages are approximately 27, 32 and 39 respectively.

coal and their capacity to perform the tasks that were to free their
masters from much drudgery depended upon the quantity of coal
that could be raised to feed them. Perhaps one reason for the comparative neglect of the history of energy consumption as providing a
grammar whose use would clarify the meaning of the industrial
revolution lies in the fact that there is an intriguing paradox in the
history of coal production in England. Despite its fundamental importance in promoting economic expansion, few if any forms of
economic activity remained so unambiguously 'pre-industrial' in
production technology for so long. Drainage and winding machinery apart, the digging of coal remained a primitive, toilsome, dirty
and dangerous matter. Coal was won by the equivalent of hoe agriculture and the wheelbarrow, by men wielding a pick and trundling
the results of their exertions to the main shaft on sleds or in small
wheeled tubs by main force, or with the assistance of pit ponies.[9] Yet
the result of the one man's efforts in the pits over a working year,
some 200 tons of coal, was to make available a quantity of energy
that utterly dwarfed what could be gained in any other way in the
working year.[10] Output per man in the pits did not change greatly
between Tudor and Edwardian times, but the importance of this
source of inanimate energy to the economy as a whole changed
dramatically.[11]

At first coal was a cheap substitute for wood as a source of heat

[9] See Flinn, *British coal industry*, pp. 91–9, for a description of the methods of coal
    extraction in the eighteenth and early nineteenth centuries.
[10] Cottrell illustrated the point in a vivid manner. 'A coal miner who consumes in his
    own body about 3,500 calories a day will, if he mines 500 pounds of coal, produce
    coal with a heat value 500 times the heat value of the food which he consumed
    while mining it. At 20 per cent efficiency he expends about 1 horsepower-hour of
    mechanical energy to get the coal. Now, if the coal he mines is burned in a steam
    engine of even 1 per cent efficiency it will yield about 27 horsepower-hours of
    mechanical energy. The surplus of mechanical energy gained would thus be 26
    horsepower-hours, or the equivalent of 26 man-days per man-day. A coal miner,
    who consumed about one-fifth as much food as a horse, could thus deliver through
    the steam engine about 4 times the mechanical energy which the average horse in
    Watt's day was found to deliver.' *Energy and society*, p. 86.
[11] Nef considered a figure of between 150 and 200 tons per miner per annum to be
    usual in the seventeenth century. Church's recent estimates suggest that in Ed-
    wardian times the comparable figure was between 250 and 300 tons. Nef, *British
    coal industry*, II, pp. 136n, 138; Church, *British coal industry*, fig. 6.1, p. 473.

energy in contexts where there was no likelihood of undesired chemical interaction between the heat source and the object heated. Thus coal could be used immediately to boil a kettle, to heat a salt pan or a dye vat, or to provide space heating, but was of little value in smelting ores because chemicals from the coal might be transferred to the resulting metal causing it to be brittle or to acquire some other undesired property. Where this risk existed, trial and error over several generations might be necessary to overcome the problem, as in the case of the smelting of iron ore where the difficulties were intricate, and two centuries were to elapse after coal use in industry had attained a significant scale before a satisfactory inorganic substitute for charcoal was found.[12] Notwithstanding such problems, both in the simpler and more complex applications of coal in industrial processes, the adoption of coal as a source of heat conferred large and increasing advantages on British industry and spurred its rate of growth.[13]

Abundant heat energy had been an increasing boon to the economy from the seventeenth century onwards, easing the pressures always present in organic economies, but to break free entirely from the constraints of such economies, it was essential to achieve the same success in the provision of mechanical energy. The history of the steam engine is too well known to call for repetition, save to point out that long before Watt was born the change which counted had already taken place. A method of deriving mechanical energy from a mineral source on a substantial scale had been discovered.

[12] There is a vivid account of this long-drawn-out process in the first four chapters of Ashton's classic early work, *Iron and steel in the industrial revolution*.

[13] In textiles, for example, Tann has enumerated the many purposes for which coal was used in increasing quantity. 'Fires were required for heating combs used in the preparation of long staple wool for worsted cloth; they were employed in the stoving process for bleaching wool and silk; for warming drying rooms for silk, wool, cotton and linen; for heating presses to finish woollen cloth and give it lustre; and for heating presses and cylinders used in the calico printing industry. But the largest quantities of fuel were required in heating the various liquids used for scouring wool and silk, bleaching cotton and linen, dyeing wool and cotton, and printing cotton and fustian. All this in addition to the rapid adoption of the steam engine by both furnace and textile industries.' Tann, 'The process industries during the industrial revolution', p. 149. The cumulative advantages conferred on British industry compared with French in the eighteenth century by use of coal are strongly emphasized by Harris, 'Industry and technology'.

The Newcomen engine was notably inefficient as a device for capturing the energy made available by the combustion of coal.[14] But since coal was cheap and its combustion released a very large quantity of heat it was even so a practicable solution to a pressing difficulty in the mining industry, that of evacuating water from mines as shafts were driven deeper and deeper to tap new coal seams.[15] It was a device dependent upon a mineral power source to solve the problems of an industry devoted to the production of a mineral raw material. However particular the problem and the solution, the result, once in being, was sure to produce fundamental change. No matter that at first the use of the device to serve other ends might strike later generations as remarkably clumsy, as when water was pumped back up from the tail race to the mill pond to keep a water wheel turning, rather than the kinetic energy being harnessed more directly. Time and ingenuity were likely to find new applications and to identify ways of securing greater efficiency once the novelty of obtaining kinetic energy from subterranean mineral beds had been shown to offer a practical means of overcoming the power problems of an important industry.[16]

[14] Its technical efficiency was only about 1–2 per cent, compared with 20 per cent for an early twentieth-century steam turbine. Cipolla, *Economic history of world population*, fig. 6, p. 57.

[15] The change of scale in the energy made available to the production process by the introduction of Newcomen engines is vividly apparent from a note by the scientist William Brownrigg following a visit to miners near Whitehaven in the early 1750s. 'It would require about 500 men, or a power equal to that of 110 horses, to work the pumps of one of the largest fire-engines (heat-engines) now in use . . . As much water may be raised by an engine of this size, kept constantly at work, as can be drawn by 2,520 men with rollers and buckets, after the manner now daily practised in many mines, or as much as can be borne upon the shoulders of twice that number of men, as is said to be done in some of the mines in Peru'. Quoted in Ubbelohde, *Man and energy*, p. 63.

[16] The significance of abundant mechanical power in heavy industry and for transport is too obvious to need emphasis; but even in lighter industries, such as textiles, it is likely that steam power was necessary for steady expansion. Well-informed contemporaries considered this to be the case. Baines, for example, writing in the 1830s thought that continued growth in the cotton industry would have been compromised, 'if a power more efficient than water had not been discovered to move the machinery. The building of mills in Lancashire must have ceased, when all the available fall of streams had been appropriated.' Baines, *Cotton manufacture*, p. 220. More recent commentators have formed the same impression. 'By 1800

Mineral-based growth

Changes in energy provision, though so important, were, of course, only one aspect of the substitution of mineral for organic raw materials across an increasing range of the production processes by which the physical needs of a community were met and its living standards determined. The developments that enabled the demand for the necessaries of life to be met without creating intolerable pressures on the land have been described. Firing and lodging escaped the old constraints first, but were eventually followed by food and clothing too. In addition other goods could be produced in such profusion that the conveniences of an earlier age came to be regarded as necessaries; and the luxuries no more than conveniences.

All metal products were once scarce and relatively costly. Iron, for instance, has many physical properties that make it of the greatest value to man but as long as the production of 10,000 tons of iron involved the felling of 100,000 acres of woodland, it was inevitable that it was used only where a few hundred-weight or at most a few tons of iron would suffice for the task in hand.[17] The strength and resilience of steel, and the precision with which it can be worked, make it an excellent material from which to make not only, say, a watch spring or a Toledo blade, but a vast range of tools and machines. But whereas the price of steel in an organic economy necessarily restricts its use severely, in a mineral-based economy machines weighing tens of tons, ships weighing thousands of tons and indeed railway track systems weighing millions of tons can all be constructed without excessive economic strain or ecological

the continued momentum of advance in strategic industries like cotton spinning and iron was dependent on enlarging the uses of the steam engine, even though only a small proportion of productive effort in the economy then depended on the engine. Everyone knew that the greatest strides in technical progress lay in applying the steam engine and iron machinery to more and more processes in more and more industries': Mathias, *First industrial nation*, p. 121.

[17] Benaerts, *La Grande Industrie allemande*, p. 454, estimated that 40,000 hectares had to be felled to produce 10,000 tons of iron products (1 hectare = approximately 2.5 acres).

disaster.[18] An iron industry whose scope for expansion must take account of the scale of present and possible future supplies of wood for charcoal is an iron industry certain to count its output in hundreds, or a best thousands of tons. Cheap mineral fuel allowed ore to be dug and converted into iron or steel on a scale that caused output to be measured by millions rather than thousands of tons.

In the new regime huge industries could develop for which the productivity of the land was an irrelevance since agricultural products did not figure amongst their raw materials – metal manufacture, machine tools and engineering; pottery, bricks, glass and ceramics; heavy and fine chemicals; shipbuilding; the manufacture of road and rail vehicles; electrical goods; most durable consumer goods industries. In many cases the transfer to sole dependence on mineral raw materials took place over a substantial period. Some recruits to the new ranks were surprising and could occur only because of major advances in scientific and technological expertise – the rubber, textile and fertilizer industries spring to mind. And the transfer in some instances affected only a part of the industry, but the cumulative effect was to substitute a new production landscape for the old with very different vistas. To use a variant of the cave myth, one might say that previously men had been chained to face the walls of a cave which appeared to circumscribe their hopes and ambitions permanently. Unlocked by the new forces at work in the economy, they were now free to turn to the mouth of the cave and luxuriate in the opportunities opening up over a vast new terrain.

The emerging pattern of increased productivity

I have developed an argument connecting the rise of what I have labelled the mineral-based energy economy with the possibility of real incomes per head making a substantial and progressive advance, and I have described two of the necessary conditions for such an advance: a radical increase in output per head facilitated by deriving from new sources far larger quantities of both heat and

---

[18] A moderate-sized railway system with 20,000 miles of single track and with rails weighing 90 lbs a yard, would require almost 3 million tons of steel for the rails alone.

mechanical energy than were previously available; and an escape from the problems associated with dependence on organic raw materials as output grew while land remained in fixed supply.

These, however, are claims about the logical status of the changes in question. The issue of their empirical realization is a different matter of equal importance to the understanding of the industrial revolution in England.

A preliminary point first. Sensational increases in output per head can only give rise to important advances in real incomes per head if they are widespread in the economy. Assuming that mobility of labour between occupations will tend to generalize the impact of any rise in production per head on real incomes, but equally that the same process will dampen any such boost according to the proportion of the workforce involved, it follows that productivity changes need to be fairly widespread to have an appreciable influence. A doubling in labour productivity confined to 1 per cent of the labour force will have a negligible effect upon overall productivity or the general level of wages. The wider the range of occupations within which productivity per head is rising, the more modest the rise required to result in any given average aggregate rise. In tracing the changes which ultimately justified using the term 'industrial revolution', therefore, it is important to pay attention to the proportion of the labour force that was drawn into jobs in which productivity was high or rising rapidly. As long as the proportion remained low the effect of the new regime, however spectacular in particular cases, was bound to remain limited.

This is a topic which would repay much more attention than it has so far received, but it seems safe to assert that, viewed in this way, the date at which the new regime began to make a substantial, general impact on English economic life was later than many accounts of the industrial revolution would suggest, and that the advanced organic economy remained the mainstay of economic life until well into the nineteenth century. It is no cause for surprise, seen in this context, that unambiguous evidence of a substantial and sustained rise in real incomes is not to be found until the middle decades of the century.

Contributions to an increase in output per head in the economy overall had come primarily from agriculture in the seventeenth and eighteenth centuries. Labour productivity in agriculture appears to have roughly doubled during that period, and agriculture was much the largest employer throughout, so that the leverage exerted by favourable changes in agricultural productivity was inevitably paramount over other influences. By 1800, however, only about 40 per cent of the adult male English labour force worked in agriculture and by 1850 the figure had declined further to no more than 25 per cent.[19] The increase in labour productivity in agriculture continued during the first half of the nineteenth century but as the weight of agriculture in the economy fell sharply, so also did the impact of productivity change in agriculture upon productivity overall. A continued upward momentum in overall productivity per head would clearly have to depend increasingly on other sectors of the economy.

Promising developments elsewhere were not lacking. In industries such as cotton and iron there was a happy combination of rapidly rising output per head and swiftly growing employment, the combination most favourable to advancing the general situation.[20] But it is important to be aware of the comparatively small numbers employed in industries of this type compared with those engaged in occupations where output per head had probably changed little for generations and was not to benefit from improved techniques for some time to come.

The first English census that provides moderately detailed information about employment is that of 1831 which covered adult males aged twenty and over in some detail, especially for those engaged in retail trades and handicraft industry. Tabulation of the data is illuminating. It so happened that Rickman, who directed the census, defined manufacturing employment, one of his seven main categories, in such a way as to include within it both men engaged in the new factories, like those erected by the cotton masters in Lancashire, and men who fitted Adam Smith's pinmakers' paradigm. The great bulk of workers in the putting-out trades, who

[19] Wrigley, 'Men on the land', tab. 11.12, p. 332. It is of interest to note that Crafts considered that total factor productivity was rising faster in agriculture than in manufacturing or in the economy generally in the period 1801–31: *British economic growth*, p. 115.

[20] Crafts has estimated that cotton alone may have accounted for half of all productivity growth in manufacturing over the period 1788–1856. Ibid., p. 85.

worked at home but whose products were sold in distant markets, those sometimes described as proto-industrial workers, were included under manufacturing. Those producing goods or services for largely local markets, on the other hand, were placed in the retail trade and handicraft category. In the former category, therefore, were to be found both men whose productivity might be expected to be rising for the reasons assigned by the classical economists, linked to increased market size and specialization of function, and men whose output per head was even more materially assisted by the use of machinery harnessed to new power sources. In the latter category, in contrast, were men whose working practices were traditional, who made little or no use of new machinery or power sources, and whose opportunities for increasing productivity by specializing in particular tasks was severely limited by the small size of the markets which they served. Changes in the length of the working day, or in the number of working days in the year, may well have been a more important cause of any increase in output per head in such employments than changes in the organization or techniques of production. It is instructive in this connection that Crafts estimated the growth in labour productivity in industry generally at only 0.4 per cent annually between 1801 and 1831.[21]

Employment in the manufacturing category amounted to only 10 per cent of adult male employment in England in 1831, and of that total more than half was to be found in Lancashire and the West Riding of Yorkshire alone; outside these two adjacent areas only one man in twenty worked in manufacturing. Employment in retail trade and handicraft, in contrast, was more than three times as large, at 32 per cent of the adult male labour force (table 3.1). The ten largest individual occupations in the retail trade and handicraft category alone employed five men for every three in manufacturing. In declining order of size they were shoemakers, carpenters, tailors, publicans, shopkeepers, blacksmiths, masons, butchers, bricklayers and bakers (table 3.2). In none of these occupational categories is it likely that output per head had been rising other than marginally for several generations past.

When allowance is made for the numbers employed in other forms

[21]   Ibid., p. 31.

Table 3.1. *Adult male employment in 1831 (twenty years of age and over)*

	No.	%
Agriculture	980,750	32.6
Manufacturing	314,106	10.4
Retail trade and handicraft	964,177	32.0
Capitalists, bankers and professionals	179,983	6.0
Labourers (other than agricultural)	500,950	16.6
Servants	70,629	2.3
Total	3,010,595	100.0

Note: in addition to the six categories shown, there was a seventh census category, 'Other males'. Overseers were instructed to return in this class any adult males not included in the other six, including, 'retired tradesmen, superannuated labourers, and males diseased or disabled in body or mind'. A total of 189,389 men were returned in this category, of whom the great bulk were probably either too old to work or physically incapacitated, so that it seems sensible to exclude them from this tabulation.
Source: 1831 Census, enumeration abstract, I, *Parliamentary Papers* 1832, xxxvi, pp. 832–3.

Table 3.2. *Major employments in retail trade and handicrafts in 1831*

Shoemakers	110,122
Carpenters	83,810
Tailors	60,166
Publicans	52,621
Shopkeepers	49,529
Blacksmiths	45,405
Masons	31,631
Butchers	31,026
Bricklayers	28,939
Bakers	23,730
Total	516,979

Source: Wrigley, 'Men on the land', tab. 11.2, pp. 300–1.

of employment where productivity was probably broadly static, such as personal service, urban labouring of all types, many clerical jobs and some types of mining, and for the probability that even within the manufacturing category there were probably many workers whose output per head was not on a rising trend, it will be obvious that the effect on overall productivity exerted by those in the forms of employment where improvement was rapid was bound to be modest. They had a large dead weight to shift.[22]

Moreover, though there was some beneficial leverage from the faster growth of employment where productivity was probably rising fastest, the differential rates of growth did not promise sudden and radical change. For example, the form in which occupational information was collected in the 1841 census makes it feasible to compare growth rates in employment over the decade between 1831 and 1841 in the two categories labelled manufacturing, and retail trade and handicraft, in the 1831 census. Predictably the rate of growth for manufacturing was the higher of the two, 4.1 per cent annually compared to 2.4 per cent, but the latter rate is still high and because the absolute number in retail trade and handicraft was so much larger at the beginning of the decade, almost two-thirds of the total growth in the two categories combined was in the category where productivity increase was probably slight, if it existed at all.[23] The building industry exemplifies this point.[24]

In considering the comparatively modest difference in the growth rates of employment in the 'modern' and 'traditional' sectors of employment, it is worth bearing in mind that in many branches of manufacturing the pressure exerted by rising productivity and falling production costs in the new factories, using new power

[22] Crafts provided upper-bound estimates of the percentage of men employed in 1841 in 'revolutionized' industries (those in which productivity was rising), and concluded that they comprised substantially less than 10 per cent of the male workforce, except in the north, and were numerous only in Lancashire and the West Riding where up to 40 per cent fell into this category: ibid., tab. 1.1, pp. 4–5, and p. 107. Crafts was also led to conclude that over the whole period total factor productivity did not grow at all outside textiles, iron manufacture, transport and agriculture. Ibid., p. 86.

[23] For details of the number of adult males in the two categories in 1831 and 1841, see Wrigley, 'Men on the land', p. 298.

[24] Crafts, British economic growth, pp. 20–2.

sources, was felt most keenly by those in 'proto-industrial' employment where the division of labour on the 'pinmakers' model had also caused some growth in productivity. Since *both* these forms of employment were counted as manufacturing in the 1831 census, the rise in numbers in the former was likely to be offset to some extent by a fall in numbers in the latter.

Admittedly, all the data quoted relate to adult males only. In some of the most dynamic industries, such as cotton textiles, a high proportion of the labour force was female, or, if male, under twenty years old. If information were available for the whole labour force, therefore, the numbers and percentages just given would be changed somewhat, probably in the direction of raising the overall percentage in forms of employment where productivity per head was rising, but not to a degree that would greatly affect the thrust of the argument presented.

The reproductive revolution

Malthus's tortoise was slowly changing in nature. It was acquiring both speed and stamina. It is time to consider how his hare was faring. Real income per head is affected by reproduction no less than production.

Malthus himself had expressed a guarded optimism, based on his knowledge of population trends in western Europe over the preceding century and a half, that the hare might be persuaded to go to sleep. Easier economic circumstances could be expected to lead to lower mortality and hence higher growth rates, though Malthus was well aware of the pronounced unhealthiness of urban life and believed many industrial pursuits to be prejudicial to good health, so that he would not have accepted such an automatic association of higher wages and reduced death rates as some of his contemporaries assumed.[25] Easier economic circumstances were also widely supposed to encourage earlier marriage and hence higher fertility, thus further increasing the speed of population growth. It was here that Malthus parted company with those who were inclined to treat such links as automatic. He considered that, encouraged and en-

---

[25] Malthus, *Essay on population* (1826), II, pp. 199, 241–3; III, pp. 441–4.

lightened by a recent experience of greater purchasing power arising from fuller employment and higher wages, those who lived by selling their labour might be so determined not to prejudice their new-found prosperity that they would exercise greater restraint in contracting marriage, would look, as he put it, 'before and after' with still more circumspection, and thus permanently alter the balance between the demand for labour and its supply, thereby allowing the enhanced standard of living to be maintained.[26]

During the first three-quarters of the nineteenth century, after falling away slightly from a peak in the growth rate at the beginning of the century, associated with exceptionally early marriage, the English population rose at a fairly steady rate close to 1.25 per cent per annum.[27] Mortality improved very little. Expectation of life at birth, for example, after rising by two or three years early in the century, stood at 40.8 years in 1831; by 1871 the figures had increased only to 41.3 years.[28] The absence of change is rather deceptive in that there were probably appreciable if modest gains in expectation of life in all areas, rural, small town, large city and metropolitan, but, because there were rapid compositional shifts within the population, taking more and more people away from relatively healthy rural and small town environments into the big cities, the net overall effect was slight.[29] Neither marital fertility nor nuptiality changed much, though the latter more than the former,[30] and although the tides of international migration ebbed and flowed irregularly, growth rates remained largely unaltered. The economic changes of the period left remarkably little mark on its demography as reflected in fertility, mortality, nuptiality or growth rates.

---

[26] Malthus, *Principles of political economy*, v, pp. 183–4.

[27] Between 1831 and 1871 the population of England rose from 13.28 million to 21.50 million, a rate of growth of 1.21 per cent per annum. Wrigley and Schofield, *Population history of England*, tab. A3.3, pp. 531–5.

[28] Ibid., tab. A3.1, pp. 528–9. The data refer to five-year periods centring on the dates given.

[29] Woods, 'The effects of population redistribution on mortality'.

[30] For marital fertility, Wrigley and Schofield, 'English population history from family reconstitution', tab. 8, p. 172 and accompanying text. For nuptiality, Wrigley and Schofield, *Population history of England*, fig. 7.15, p. 262, tab. 10.1, p. 424, and tabs. 10.3 and 10.4, p. 437. As will be seen from these data there was a moderate fall in nuptiality early in the century but very little change thereafter.

In the last quarter of the century, however, not only did the chief measures of demographic behaviour begin a period of radical change but, more fundamentally, the old assumptions about the relationship between economic and demographic variables began to be falsified. Continued, and indeed accelerated, improvements in mortality were to be expected on traditional assumptions. Living standards were rising, and by a variety of causal paths, both direct and indirect, there was every reason to expect death rates to fall. In this respect events followed the expected pattern. The speed and extent of the fall was without precedent but at least the direction of movement was predictable.[31] Wealth and health went hand in hand. *Ceteris paribus* population growth rates should have risen as a result.

In conformity with the old verities the acceleration associated with reduced mortality should have been further boosted by a rise in fertility. The classical economists had taken it for granted that better wages would lead to earlier marriage, larger families and so faster growth. The demand for labour must secure a matching supply. There was plenty of scope for fertility to increase, since the mean age at marriage for women was fairly high, and a substantial proportion of each cohort remained single throughout life.[32] But a doubly-new pattern gradually appeared over the two generations after 1870. Greater prosperity did not lead to earlier or more universal marriage: if anything marriage age rose and celibacy increased down to the outbreak of the First World War.[33] But a second and far more radical break from the past was also taking place. Nuptiality change was ceasing to play the leading role in altering fertility. Fertility change occurred *within* marriage rather than *by* marriage as the practice of birth control spread more and more widely through the population until by the 1930s large families had become a rarity: more than half

[31] Expectation of life at birth rose steadily after 1871, reaching 43.8 in 1891, 51.3 in 1911, 60.2 in 1931 and 68.3 in 1951. Preston, Keyfitz and Schoen, *Causes of death*, pp. 236–63. These figures were obtained by combining data for males and females on the assumption that the sex ratio at birth was 105:100.

[32] For an illustration of the extent to which changes in nuptiality could alter growth rates, *ceteris paribus*, see Wrigley and Schofield, *Population history of England*, pp. 266–9. The exercise demonstrated that the changes in nuptiality occurring between the late seventeenth and early nineteenth centuries were sufficient to have increased the intrinsic growth rate by about 1.25 per cent per annum.

[33] Wrigley and Schofield, *Population history of England*, pp. 435–8.

of all couples had either one child or two children, and most of the remainder either none or three children.[34] Whereas under the old system greater prosperity, through its effect on nuptiality, tended to raise fertility, under the new dispensation, with individual couples exercising discretion over the size of their families, if anything the relationship was reversed. The hare no longer chose to run free: his gait grew very sedate.

The acquisition by the tortoise of both stamina and speed were closely related developments. The essence of the former was to escape dependence upon the products of the land whose quantity could not be expanded indefinitely as long as farms were ecologically self-sufficient units. This ensured that the process of growth at a relatively high rate could be sustained over a very long period. The key change that ensured the latter was the tapping of a new store of energy capital, so abundant that its production could be expanded immensely without causing any immediate problems of exhaustion of the energy stock. Access to abundant energy stocks was initially of limited value because the new sources of energy could be used only to provide heat, but once a method had been devised for deriving mechanical work also from the new energy source, the way was clear for individual productivity to make a quantum leap. The tortoise could now sprint rather than crawl. Production could outpace population.

In conformity with past experience the same changes that transformed the tortoise might also have been expected to increase the speed of the hare, pushing it closer to the growth rate ceiling set by biological factors. Biology prescribes a minimum average interval between births and a minimum rate of depletion by death in human populations. These two constraints in turn, by defining a fertility maximum and a mortality minimum, set a limit to the attainable population growth rate. In the event mortality trends moved in the expected direction, but fertility trends did not. Rather than moving further and further apart in response to greater prosperity, mortality and fertility converged. Population growth died away. Great efforts have been made to explain convincingly the association between rising prosperity and the exercise of parental choice in favour of

[34] Wrigley, *Population and history*, tab. 5.18, p. 198.

small families, and some plausible hypotheses have been advanced in that connection, but the causes of the radical change in fertility remain unclear and open to dispute.[35] The comparative timing of the change presents a dual problem – both that over so much of Europe it should have been so nearly simultaneous even though the extent of economic and social change varied greatly, and that in parts of one country, France, there should have been major declines in marital fertility long before there was any alteration in the traditional rhythms of an organic economy.[36]

Whatever the *cause* of the change, however, its *effect* was of profound importance. Had the rate of population growth prevailing about 1870 continued, the population of England by the year 2000 would have reached about 110 million, roughly double the prospective total at that date. If mortality had followed its historic path, but fertility had remained at its level in 1870 or had risen, the pattern to be expected in terms of earlier experience, the population would have reached a far higher total still. While the effect of higher population growth rates upon living standards, judged in purely economic terms, remains a matter of dispute, it is reasonable to suppose that conditions of life viewed more generally would have suffered from population growth on such a scale. The disconnection of population growth trends from economic growth rates has, among other things, removed many of the terrors from the prospect of a slowing of economic growth.

Misunderstanding proto-industrialization

I have retold the story of the industrial revolution as a tale of two capitalisms, one connoting the kind of changes in economy and

[35] Amongst recent attempts to grapple with this issue may be mentioned, Bulatao and Lee, *Determinants of fertility*; Caldwell, *Theory of fertility decline*; Schultz, *Economics of population*; Andorka, *Determinants of fertility*; Easterlin, 'The economics and sociology of fertility'; Becker, *A treatise on the family*; and for a sceptical review of most theorizing, see Cleland and Wilson, 'Demand theories of the fertility transition'. See also United Nations, *Determinants and consequences of population trends*.

[36] For data about the fertility decline in different countries, Chesnais, *La Transition démographique*; for a general description and discussion of the concept of the fertility transition, Andorka, *Determinants of fertility*; for the particular case of France, Wrigley, 'Marital fertility in nineteenth-century France'.

society which engaged the attention of Adam Smith, the other
bound up with the questions that concerned Jevons; the one related
to growth by specialization of function, the other to the successful
harnessing of new sources of heat and mechanical energy in the
productive process, and to the substitution of mineral for organic
raw materials. Recognizing these distinctions suggests reassessment
of some topics that have received much attention and aroused controversy in recent years. Take, for example, the alleged tendency of
capitalism, in the usual meaning of the term, to increase the poverty
of the poor while adding to the wealth of the rich. Sometimes a
semi-technical word is used to describe the process, immiseration.
Those who are rendered dependent solely upon the sale of their
labour for their sustenance suffer, while those who own the capital
which sets them on work prosper. In recent years the debate has
been broadened and enriched by the introduction of the concept of
proto-industrialization.

Proto-industrialization connotes a system in which the product
continues to be manufactured domestically, often with little or no
change in production techniques, but the individual producer ceases
to be an independent small master. The material on which he works
is put out to him by a capitalist middleman who pays him to carry
out a stage in the manufacturing process. In time he may not only
cease to own the material on which he works but the machine which
he employs. Thus the framework knitters of Leicestershire were increasingly often unable to muster sufficient capital to buy a stocking
frame and were obliged instead to rent it from the same capitalist
who supplied the yarn to be knitted.[37] It is usually regarded as an
essential element of proto-industrializsation that the product is sold
in a distant, often an international, market. The worker therefore
loses any direct contact with the market in which the goods he
produces are sold, and with it any possibility of influencing the behaviour of the market. He becomes exposed to the vagaries of the trade
cycle and war. Where production and the point of sale are widely
divorced in space and transport is slow, only an entrepreneur with a
significant capital can finance the substantial interval of time that
must elapse between the outlay on raw material and the ultimate

[37] Levine, *Family formation in an age of nascent capitalism*, ch. 2.

return from sale in distant markets, an interval that may last for many months.[38] The process of production, however, may well lend itself to the kind of gains in productivity that Adam Smith had in mind in telling the parable of the pinmakers, and the product can therefore often undercut other types of manufacture.

The proponents of the concept of proto-industrialization often effect a marriage of Malthus and Marx, regarding the structural changes in economic relations involved as a long step towards a pure proletariat while at the same time laying great emphasis on the importance of the breakdown of traditional constraints on early marriage as a major reason for the immiseration of proto-industrial workers.[39] Mendels, the progenitor of the concept, described a ratchet-like process by which marriage age might be successively lowered without any compensating movements in the opposite direction.[40]

Both the empirical accuracy and the theoretical validity of the concept of proto-industrialization have been called in question,[41] and it would be a digression from my theme to enter this debate, but it is worth noting that its appearance changes considerably if it is given a different context. Within the confines of an organic economy, as we have seen, the process of economic growth is very likely to provoke problems if long sustained. Nor is there sound reason for optimism in the long term about the course of real wages. The pattern sometimes regarded as characteristic of a proto-industrializing community, in which there is an initial period of relatively high earnings followed a couple of generations later by more and more severe pressure on earnings because the labour market has become oversupplied, epitomizes in miniature the general tendencies inherent in expansion in an organic economy. Such pressure becomes especially severe if the inherent problems are exaggerated by a partial failure in the demographic mechanisms that usually preserve a tolerable equilibrium between production

[38] The term proto-industrialization was coined by Mendels and the concept was first described by him in 'Proto-industrialization'.
[39] Medick, 'Population development under the proto-industrial system'.
[40] Mendels, 'Industrialization and population pressure'.
[41] See, for example, Coleman, 'Proto-industrialization'; Houston and Snell, 'Proto-industrialization?'; and Ogilvie, 'Corporatism and regulation'.

and reproduction. One of the provinces of The Netherlands provides a classic example of a cycle of this type, which contributed to Dutch economic problems in the later eighteenth century no less than did the contemporary problems of energy supply. Slicher van Bath's monograph on Overijssel shows vividly how great were the sufferings in the textile industry as population grew rapidly but market demand failed to keep pace. Poverty and unemployment were widespread and many turned to the potato as a food staple, unable to continue to eat the more expensive cereal foods.[42]

It was not the capitalist nature of the proto-industrial system that produced pressure on living standards, but the inherent difficulties associated with economic growth in an organic economy. Equally, it was not the capitalist nature of the English economy in the nineteenth century that eventually led to rising living standards for all classes. Capitalism in the traditional sense of the term is consonant with either eventuality. It was the fact that the nineteenth-century English economy was capitalist in the second sense in which I have used the term that made the essential difference. In the process it often caused peculiarly severe problems for proto-industrial areas. The death throes of the Belgian domestic linen industry in the 1840s, for example, were brought about by the competition of factory production in English mills.[43] Capitalism as normally understood, for the reasons set out in the *Wealth of nations*, may be capable of leading to a better allocation of resources, and, by facilitating specialization of function, may lead to rising output per head in many sectors of the economy, but, again for reasons explained by Adam Smith and further elaborated by Ricardo and Malthus, the cumulative effect of the changes may prove to be neutral or even adverse with respect to the real incomes of the bulk of the population. The only upshot of the growth process in a capitalist economy defined in the classical manner that would have greatly surprised those who first examined its nature was what ultimately occurred: a major, progressive, sustained rise in real incomes spread throughout the community.

[42] Slicher van Bath, *Een samenleving onder spanning*, pp. 352–68, 566–79.
[43] Jacquemyns, *La Crise économique des Flandres*, esp. chs. 2 and 3.

Conclusion

The transition from an advanced organic to an energy-based mineral economy was long-drawn-out. In the sense that mineral sources of heat energy began to replace earlier alternatives as early as the later sixteenth century on an appreciable scale, it was under way in Tudor times. In the sense that productivity changes closely linked to the use of the new sources of mechanical energy were still affecting only a small faction of the labour force at the end of the first third of the nineteenth century, a largely organic economy continued as the dominant mode until well into that century. That the trend in real income per head should have been uncertain until such a late date is not surprising. If real income is treated as the key defining characteristic of the industrial revolution, then it follows that the latter also was not unambiguously established until the second half of the nineteenth century.

But these are somewhat abstract considerations. If the new categories used and distinctions drawn have a virtue, it is in enabling old issues to be reviewed with a fresh eye. It is patently mistaken to expect to find a 'before' situation with little or no growth, followed after a brief transitional stage by an 'after' situation with strong, consistent growth; nor, indeed, is such a view often advanced. But some methods of measurement and analysis may induce an opposite kind of problem. If, for example, explanation is made to depend heavily on a model in which the level of net investment as a proportion of national income is regarded as a key variable, and if the percentage in question shows little sign of change over time, puzzlement may result.[44] Much the same is true, *mutatis mutandis* of over-reliance on simple aggregate measures such as the gross national

[44] The view that the key to growth lies in increasing sharply the proportion of national income devoted to net investment was set out forcefully by Lewis, *Economic growth*, esp. ch. 5. He viewed a rise from 5 to 12 per cent as representing the order of magnitude of increase needed to produce an industrial revolution. A few years later Deane and Cole ventured cautiously into the question of the extent of any acceleration in the percentage of national income used for investment during the English industrial revolution. They suggested in 1962 that the percentage rose from 5–6 per cent before 1780 to about 7 per cent by 1800, but thereafter that it stagnated or declined during the war period, and only rose again significant-

product. The key point about organic economies was not that in them growth was impossible or was necessarily slight. Where an institutional framework favouring growth existed or could be brought into being substantial growth could occur. It was this type of growth and the circumstances which favoured it which the classical economists described and analysed with such conspicuous elegance. It might be reflected in measures of aggregate advance in a manner difficult to distinguish from the patterns visible in the later period when the material base of the economy had been transformed. But the secular prospects for growth of the type that could occur in an organic economy were very different from those to which recent generations have become accustomed. The classical economists not only regarded growth as necessarily bounded but considered that it was the growth process itself which ensured that the inherent limitations associated with it would begin to bite.

If the views of the classical economists about the approach of the stationary state were justified in terms of the economies with which they were familiar; if this was a world in which negative feedback must be expected finally to prevail; if the tension between production

ly after 1830, by 3 per cent between 1830 and 1860; Deane and Cole, *British economic growth*, pp. 263–4. When Feinstein turned his attention to this issue, he did so on the basis of a greatly enlarged body of empirical work, and concluded in 1978 that total domestic investment expressed as a proportion of gross domestic product rose from 8 per cent in the 1760s to a plateau of 12 per cent in the decades between 1820 and 1850. Still more recently, in 1985, Crafts has attacked the issue once again, and has produced estimates that come closer to Lewis's 'model'. Crafts's estimate of the same measure of investment used by Feinstein shows the investment proportion rising from 6 to 12 per cent between 1760 and 1830, but more smoothly than Feinstein's estimates, for Feinstein's work suggested that the rise was concentrated into the period between the 1760s and the 1790s. Feinstein, 'Capital formation in Great Britain', tab. 28, p. 91; Crafts, *British economic growth*, tab. 4.1, p. 73. Feinstein has recently reworked his capital formation estimates; his revision reduces the extent of the rise in investment percentages published earlier. See also table 4.2 below.

Reflecting on both evidence about and analysis of the industrial revolution McCloskey recently wrote, 'rises in income that are not explicable as more machines per man dominate the story. This is a bitter disappointment to economists. The scientists of scarcity delight in the thought that more consumption later can come only from abstinence now. As it is put in the mildly comical jargon of the discipline, there is no such thing as a free lunch. Yet indubitably Britain from 1780 to 1860 ate a massive free lunch.' McCloskey, 'Industrial revolution', p. 65.

and reproduction denied the hope of success to all but the most modest expectations about the course of real wages in the future, then there was a major disjunction between the old and the new, not to be resolved into a change in the investment ratio or a continuation and accentuation of patterns long established, and apt to remain concealed if sought only by the conventional tools of economic analysis. Time was to prove that the classical economists were mistaken in their views about the future. Growth was more nearly exponential than asymptotic. The principle of diminishing marginal returns did not gradually strangle the growth process. The tension between production and reproduction gradually relaxed. The world for the first time moved into an era when Jesus's remark at the house of Simon the leper, 'ye have the poor always with you'[45] ceased to be a truism, made certain by the inherent feebleness of man's productive powers, and became a problematic statement. Poverty became in a sense a matter of choice. The capacity to alleviate it now existed, as Marx recognized. For the first time it was becoming a practical issue rather than a matter for utopian suggestion to discuss whether the scourge of poverty could be eliminated if the greatly enhanced powers of production were applied with vigour and their fruits distributed appropriately.

[45] Matthew, 26.11. The phraseology is that of the King James bible.

4

Numbers and notions

In her recent study of poverty, Himmelfarb wrote that the industrial revolution was 'presumably reflected' in the *Wealth of nations*, adding that the effect of Adam Smith's great book, 'was to give technology and industry a new and decisive role not only in the economy but in society. The division of labour . . . became the harbinger of a social revolution as momentous as anything dreamed of by political reformers and revolutionaries.'[1] The fact that these remarks were not central to the main theme of her argument enhances their value for my purposes. They may be taken to represent a common view of the nature of the key analytic concept to be used in apprehending the industrial revolution, and of its significance in the writings of contemporary economists, of whom Adam Smith, frequently depicted as the most authoritative and articulate advocate of the capitalist system, was the most weighty.[2]

The thinking that lies behind the view Himmelfarb expressed has several characteristic components. Proximately, economic advance occurs because increased market size permits specialization of function and hence rising productivity per head. The process also involves, and indeed is conditional upon, better transport facilities and more sophisticated commercial methods and financial instru-

---

[1] Himmelfarb, *The idea of poverty*, p. 44.
[2] Rostow has noted much the same point. 'Adam Smith and Karl Marx implanted in all our minds the notion that, somehow, the industrial revolution flowed in an automatic way from the commercial revolution, via the expansion of markets in the one case, the enlargement of a middle class in the other.' Rostow, *How it all began*, p. 225.

ments. It induces urban growth and more effective integration of settlements of all sizes into an articulated urban hierarchy. Its character is such that it requires a rising quantity of circulating capital to sustain commercial operations on a new and larger scale conducted routinely over much greater distances, and, after a time, will also require more fixed capital as the level of economic activity rises to justify investment in machinery, warehouses, bridges, harbours, ships, carts, roads, mills and mines. The set of related developments is best exemplified in manufacturing industry and in transport. In agriculture the circumstances of production may limit the degree to which labour can become specialized, but here too there are comparable changes. Better transport and larger markets, for example, combine to make it feasible for each region to abandon local self-sufficiency without running the risk of starvation, and enable an area well suited to, say, stock raising largely to abandon grain growing, in the knowledge that the fattened stock will find a market and that the resultant increased flow of income will secure grain at prices below local production costs. The whole complex of advances is conceived as mutually reinforcing, so that a momentum of change once established may gather pace as time passes.

The concept of modernization

Analysis may stop at this level, but equally it may extend to what are seen as more basic changes in the society in question. We are sometimes provided, for example, with a check list of changes which jointly imply the transition from a traditional to a modern society, and will generate the kind of economic developments just described, the development as a whole being termed modernization. The twin, key notions underpinning the concept of modernization are rationality and self-interest. Both are given a semi-technical meaning. By rational behaviour is meant action which tends to maximize the economic returns to the individual or group called upon to make a decision and implement it. There are, of course, utilities which might be maximized other than those that are economic, and in traditional societies they may be given preference, but in the course of modernization such non-economic preferences become subordinate to economic imperatives. For example, to revert to a situation mentioned earlier, it may be perfectly rational in the general sense of the term to decide to retain a son on a holding even though his marginal product is less than his consumption because the preservation of the family as an integral unit is seen as more important than maximizing average incomes, but in the technical sense to do so would qualify as an irrational decision.[3]

Similarly, self-interest is held to be the guiding principle of action in a modernized society to a degree that might appear both aberrant and abhorrent in traditional communities. Once again, in the general sense of the term, self-interest may be as conspicuous a guiding principle of action in a traditional society as in a modern, industrial one. Indeed one might argue that it must be difficult in principle to imagine individual actions not largely actuated by self-interest. In a traditional society a man may devote much of his time and energy to promoting the well-being, security and status of his relatives, his fellow villagers, his lord or his dependents and yet be acting from self-interest. But self-interest in the context of modernization theory has come to mean the adoption of a calculus of advantage in which the unit is the individual himself and the accounting scale is pecuniary gain.

The concepts of rationality and self-interest are buttressed by a number of subsidiary indicators of change in the direction of modernization – the replacement of ascription by achievement as the basis of recruitment to office; the substitution of universalistic for particularistic criteria for membership of all kinds of groups, societies and associations; the spread of functional specificity in place of functional diffuseness; and so on. The furtherance of such changes also implies movement towards a characteristic form and mode of operation of the legal system; towards a particular definition of the scope, nature and stability of property rights; and perhaps also to the development of the nation-state, exercising sovereignty, employing bureaucratic techniques of government and acting in harmony with the interests of the bourgeoisie. In some analyses, the changes in relationships between individuals that modernization entails are paralleled by change within them. For individuals to act effectively in

---

[3] The arguments and descriptions summarized in this discussion of modernization may be found, set out at greater length, in Wrigley, 'Modernization and the industrial revolution in England'.

a modernized society, for example, they are pictured as needing to achieve much greater autonomy than is appropriate in traditional society with the disappearance of authority figures that were once perceived as protective and nurturant.

The move along the spectrum from traditional to modern may also be pictured in other terms as from *Gemeinschaft* to *Gesellschaft*, or from feudal to capitalist. Sometimes the analytic framework in the latter case may be Marxist but there is a considerable area of common ground in relation to these issues between Marxist and non-Marxist analyses. No one captured the ethos of the new age more vividly than Adam Smith. In a much-quoted passage that will bear a further repetition, he wrote:

man has almost constant occasion for the help of his brethren, and it is in vain for him to expect it from their benevolence only. He will be more likely to prevail if he can interest their self-love in his favour, and show them that it is for their own advantage to do for him what he requires of them . . . It is not from the benevolence of the butcher, the brewer, or the baker that we expect our dinner, but from their regard to their own interest. We address ourselves, not to their humanity but to their self-love, and never talk of our own necessities but of their advantages. Nobody but a beggar chooses to depend chiefly upon the benevolence of his fellow-citizens.[4]

It is common to all such typologies of transition to regard the change from early Tudor to late Victorian England and beyond as movement along a single spectrum, the working out amid the vagaries of time and place of a continuous and progressive change, in which the later stages in the transformation are implicit in those that had gone before. In some cases the industrial revolution is explicitly regarded as a natural concomitant of the later stages of the transition, requiring no special explanation because it represented the logical culmination of the economic side of modernization, the fruit of the gains in productivity that flowed from changes in the institutional structure of society, in its ethos, in its locus of political power and, more immediately, from the economic benefits of rational conduct leading to such helpful new features as greater specialization of economic function. To eliminate any apparent incongruity between a long process of progressive change in in-

[4] Smith, *Wealth of nations*, ed. Cannan, I, p. 18.

stitutional forms and social behaviour on the one hand, and a much briefer period of violent economic transformation on the other, Geertz suggested the existence of a process rather like the heating of water in a kettle, which may culminate suddenly with the lid blowing off but only because the water has reached a critical temperature and turned to steam after a much longer and slower heating process.[5]

In my view this model of the transition in its many variant forms is of dubious validity. There may be no reason to challenge the view that the advent of a system with some or all of the attributes that have been listed will increase both aggregate output and, at least for a time, output per head. If a congeries of the underlying changes can be identified that is most helpfully defined as capitalist, then it is also fair to associate the concept of capitalism with the proximate economic changes. But it is a very large additional step to regard the industrial revolution as a further natural stage in the progressive development of the phenomenon.

Modernization and the industrial revolution in England

English history appears at first blush to afford support for the view that the modernization process culminated abruptly in an industrial revolution. It is plausible to suggest that England developed unusually early as a nation-state; that many of the economic and political characteristics of feudalism faded early from the scene; that, especially in agriculture, capitalist organization spread rapidly and met remarkably little resistance; that legal institutions and practice facilitated the replacement of custom by contract; that particularistic attitudes were less prominent and less durable than in many other countries; and, of course, that economic progress was unusually rapid. It is clear that most of these changes were progressive and had reached an advanced stage by the later eighteenth century, and it is

---

[5] He wrote, 'Though it may be true that, as an economic process development is a dramatic, revolutionary change, as a broadly social process it fairly clearly is not. What looks like a quantum jump from a specifically economic point of view is, from a generally social one, merely the final expression in economic terms of a process which has been building up gradually over an extended period of time.' Geertz, *Peddlers and princes*, p. 2.

not in dispute that the industrial revolution was an English phenomenon in the first instance.

Yet there is strong historical evidence casting doubt on any automatic association of the characteristics often grouped under the descriptive label of modernization with the industrial revolution, and there are also cogent theoretical considerations pointing away from the conclusion so often drawn.

The historical evidence relates to the Dutch Republic. Except that the Dutch provinces retained substantial autonomy, calling in question the cohesiveness of Holland as a nation-state, Holland was perhaps more completely 'modern' than England throughout the period from, say, 1550 to 1750. Specialization of economic function was far advanced at an early date in both industry and agriculture. Holland possessed a custom-made internal transport network superior to anything to be found in England, and the envy of those foreigners who made use of it. She was the common carrier of Europe. Her cities were numerous and prosperous, and the percentage of the population living in towns was higher than in England and far higher than in most other countries.[6] The bourgeoisie possessed great political influence. Capitalism was perhaps less impeded by legal and institutional handicaps than anywhere else. Real wages were the highest in Europe throughout the later sixteenth and seventeenth centuries, and for much of the eighteenth century also.[7] And yet there was no early industrial revolution in Holland: indeed it was unusually late in making an appearance there.

This empirical fact is not surprising when set against the theoretical considerations disjoining the modernization process from the industrial revolution. There are few if any features present in modernization theory that are not to be found foreshadowed in the *Wealth of nations*, allowing for the differing modes of expression,[8] yet neither Adam Smith nor the other classical economists believed the

---

[6] In 1675 approximately 38 per cent of the Dutch population lived in towns of 5,000 inhabitants or more: at about the same date the comparable English figure was 14 per cent; the French 10 per cent. Wrigley, 'Urban growth and agricultural change', tab. 2, p. 128, tab. 8, p. 154, tab. 9, pp. 158–9.

[7] De Vries, 'Decline and rise of the Dutch economy', esp. pp. 173–85.

[8] Wrigley, 'Modernization and the industrial revolution in England'.

prospects for further economic growth to be very inviting. Both the experience of Holland and general considerations bearing upon the constraints to growth cautioned against supposing growth would continue for very long or that the standard of living of the bulk of the population would rise. A technically perfect capitalism appeared to be as easily consonant with the stationary state as with continuous, rapid growth. Something more than modernization or capitalism in the usual meaning of the term was needed to enable England to escape the same fate as Holland and to become the first country in which the age-old constraints on growth lost their force, the country where in spite of the forebodings of some contemporaries, it became clear that poverty was not the inevitable fate of the bulk of the population, nor a sweating brow the precondition of a daily loaf.

The transition that produced the change in prospects was the move from an advanced organic to a mineral-based energy economy. Such a move was essential if the problems so succinctly analysed by Ricardo were not to put a stop to growth sooner or later; nor could the tension exposed by Malthus's *Essay on population* be overcome without it. A different sort of capitalism was required, in alliance with the familiar variety, if the limitations inherent in all organic economies were to be overcome. Above all, a source of energy was needed whose scale would make feasible a rise in output per worker which remained beyond reach as long as his own muscles and those of his domesticated animals were almost the sole means of lifting, pulling, moving, beating, stretching and pressing material objects; and as long as he was dependent upon organic raw materials for all purposes, including that of raising heat. Such an energy source was not be found within the confines of an organic economy. The nature of both types of economy has already been described. The distinction between the two capitalisms has been outlined, and some implications of the distinction examined, for example in relation to the concept of proto-industrialisation. If there is merit in the suggestion that the difference between the advanced organic and the mineral-based energy economy was great and that the transition from one to the other was little to be expected, some further reflections suggest themselves in relation to the industrial revolution in England.

The changing balance of investment

First, there are dangers in the use of some types of quantitative data. Aggregate measures, say of gross national product, may conceal as much as they reveal. That substantial growth was possible within the confines of an organic economy is clear, and that the initial impact of the economy of the move to a different basis was modest is also clear. It is quite possible, therefore, that a smooth path traced out in, say, annual aggregate growth rates, may consist both of an element associated with the kind of growth possible in an advanced organic regime and of an element associated with the new sources of growth. In that case, the former would initially be the dominant factor in the overall growth rate but its share would fall gradually as the latter increased in importance. Compositional change of this kind is easily lost in general measures. Estimates of capital formation and its constituent elements provide a telling illustration of the complexities that can attend a breakdown of aggregate measures.

When Deane and Cole turned their attention to this issue a few years after Lewis's emphasis upon the importance of an increase in the proportion of national income devoted to investment, they concluded tentatively that the percentage rose slowly and modestly in Britain from 5 to 6 per cent before 1780 to about 7 per cent by 1800, with little further change until 1830, after which a more considerable rise of about 3 per cent or more took place, raising the level to at least 10 per cent over the next three decades.[9] Later, Feinstein published a more elaborate series of estimates based on much detailed empirical work relating to investment in each major industrial category, while Crafts has quite recently produced a further series. These last two estimates are shown in table 4.1.

As Crafts explained when comparing his estimates with those of Feinstein,[10] a main reason for the substantially lower level of his estimates in the early decades of the period covered was that he considered that the rate of growth of gross national product was substantially slower between 1760 and 1830 than Deane and Cole had supposed (Feinstein had used their estimates in a modified form

[9] Deane and Cole, *British economic growth*, pp. 263–4; see also p. 95 n. 44.
[10] Crafts, *British economic growth*, p. 72.

Table 4.1. *Gross domestic investment as a per-*
centage share of gross national product

	Feinstein		Crafts
1761–70	8.0	1760	6.0
1771–80	9.0		
1781–90	12.0	1780	7.0
1791–1800	13.0		
1801–10	11.0	1801	7.9
1811–20	11.0	1811	8.5
1821–30	12.0	1821	11.2
		1831	11.7

Note: Feinstein's percentages relate to gross domestic
product but, following Crafts, the two series are here
treated as comparable.
Sources: Feinstein, 'Capital formation in Great Britain',
tab. 28, p. 91; Crafts, *British economic growth*, tab. 4.1, p.
73.

in calculating his investment percentages[11]). Of necessity, therefore,
since the two series converge on very similar estimates by 1830,
Crafts's estimates will be lower at the beginning of the period.
Though the scale and timing of the rise in the investment percentages differ significantly, however, with rather different implications
for the validity of Lewis's thesis about the role of investment in
securing accelerated growth, it is only when the aggregates are de-
composed that several striking features of the character of the industrial revolution come to light.

Feinstein's first capital formation estimates, used in table 4.1,
have been modified by his later investigations. The aggregate series
is now modestly higher in the early decades and somewhat lower in
the later, and he has provided a changed and fuller sectoral breakdown of the overall investment totals. The revised estimates provided
the data used in calculating the percentages set out in table 4.2
which divides the decadal investment totals into four main categories.[12]

[11] Feinstein, 'Capital formation in Great Britain', tab. 25, p. 84.
[12] Feinstein, 'National totals, 1750–1920'.

Table 4.2. *Percentage distribution of gross domestic fixed capital formation in major categories*

	1761–70	1771–80	1781–90	1791–1800	1801–10	1811–20	1821–30	1831–40	1841–50	1851–60
Feinstein's revised estimates										
Agriculture	31.0	29.3	30.9	32.1	26.2	24.3	17.1	14.1	13.7	13.5
Mineral-based industries	10.2	9.6	13.4	11.4	13.8	14.3	21.7	31.1	50.7	43.2
Residental dwellings	20.7	23.1	21.5	20.6	23.9	26.9	28.7	25.0	13.5	16.1
Other industries, services	38.1	38.0	34.2	35.9	36.1	34.5	32.5	29.8	22.1	27.2
Total	100.0	100.0	100.0	100.0	100.0	100.0	100.0	100.0	100.0	100.0
Feinstein's revised estimates excluding residental dwellings										
Agriculture	39.0	38.1	39.4	40.4	34.4	33.2	24.0	18.8	15.8	16.1
Mineral-based industries	12.9	12.5	17.1	14.4	18.1	19.6	30.4	41.5	58.6	51.5
Other industries, services	48.0	49.4	43.6	45.2	47.4	47.2	45.6	39.7	25.5	32.4
Total	100.0	100.0	100.0	100.0	100.0	100.0	100.0	100.0	100.0	100.0

Note: for details of the industries comprising the categories 'Mineral-based industries', and 'Other industries, services', see accompanying text.

Source: Feinstein, 'National totals, 1750–1920'.

Feinstein used eighteen subdivisions in his revised estimates, of which two, agriculture and residential dwellings, are used unchanged in table 4.2, but the other sixteen have been collapsed into only two further groupings, one comprising the industries especially closely related to the new mineral-based energy economy, and the other all the rest. The former consists of mining and quarrying; manufacturing and construction; gas supply; and railways. The latter comprises a transport and communications group (subdivided into roads and bridges; goods and passenger transport; docks and harbours; ships; and post office, telephones and telegraphy); a group described as public and social services (with four sub-heads, educational; medical and poor law; religious; and sewerage and other public services); distribution and other services; and water supply. These are the four groupings used in the upper panel of table 4.2.

Needless to say, the investment categories grouped together as reflecting the growth of a mineral-based energy economy are an imperfect reflection of what they are intended to measure. Mining and quarrying presents no problem. It is an explicitly mineral category, dominated by coal, the key raw material of the new age. Equally, railways and gas are unambiguously 'mineral' in nature. On the other hand, manufacturing and construction is both the largest element in the group (except in the 1840s) and miscellaneous in nature. In the early decades it will have included a significant proportion of investment in industries using organic raw materials, and not using the new sources of energy. Some major industries remained 'hybrid' in this respect, either for a time or permanently. Cotton factories afford a good example of the latter possibility. The initial percentage for mineral-related investments is therefore probably too high relative to the final figure. However, there can be no reasonable doubt that the balance in industrial investment as a whole was shifting, so far as construction, machinery and power supply were concerned, in ways that ensured that well before the end of the period the great bulk of industrial investment fell squarely into the mineral-based, energy-consuming category to which manufacturing and construction have been allocated. There are also problems of the opposite kind. Some investment that was mineral-related has been excluded from its appropriate category. For example, iron ships had made an appearance in transport before the end of the period, and both sewerage and water supply systems might plausibly have been included.

Whatever the crudity of the categorization, however, the radical shifts in the proportion of investment in the several groups is clear. The share of agriculture, the necessary foundation of almost all material production in an organic economy, fell from about 31 per cent in the last four decades of the eighteenth century to only 13.5 per cent in 1851–60, while the proportion of the total devoted to forms of investment closely linked to the new mineral-based energy economy rose from only about 11 per cent in the closing decades of the eighteenth century to a maximum of over 50 per cent in the 1840s. If investment in residential dwellings is excluded from the total, because it was always a substantial but also a somewhat variable element, strongly affected by demographic factors, and because the link between the level of investment and increased productive capacity is much less direct in the case of housing than with other forms of investment, then the two sets of percentages change to those shown in the lower panel of table 4.2. Calculated in this fashion, over the first four decades the share of agriculture averaged 39.2 per cent while that of the new mineral-based energy economy averaged 14.2 per cent; in the last three decades of the period the two average percentages were 16.9 and 50.5

Such percentages suggest dramatic change, where the aggregate investment percentage changes, shown in table 4.1, were quite modest, yet the pattern shown in table 4.2 can also be misleading. It reveals a striking alteration in the proportional investment shares of two of the main categories, but casts no light on the percentages of gross national product involved. Table 4.3 attacks this further topic. In it Feinstein's revised figures were again used but, in order to take account of the revisionist view of GNP trends that detects slower growth in the late eighteenth and early nineteenth centuries than was once supposed, his estimates of gross domestic fixed capital formation have been related to Crafts's estimates of GNP.[13] Crafts accepts Feinstein's investment estimates as accurate: their differen-

---

[13] It is of interest to note Crafts's view of investment in the period 1760–1820. 'Increases in investment were required to cope with extra population pressure triggered off by economic growth in the late pre-industrial revolution period, and in the period down to the 1820s the contribution of higher investment rates was essentially to prevent the capital-to-labour ratio from *falling* and thus tending adversely to affect income per head.' Crafts, *British economic growth*, pp. 77–8.

Table 4.3. *Gross domestic fixed capital formation as a percentage share of gross domestic product*

	(1) Total	(2) Agriculture	(3) Mineral-based industries	(4) Residential dwellings	(5) (1) − (3)	(6) (1) − (3 + 4)
1761–70	6.0	1.9	0.6	1.3	5.4	4.1
1771–80	6.9	2.0	0.7	1.6	6.2	4.6
1781–90	6.2	1.9	0.8	1.3	5.4	4.1
1791–1800	6.1	2.0	0.7	1.3	5.4	4.1
1801–10	7.4	1.9	1.0	1.8	6.4	4.6
1811–20	8.4	2.0	1.2	2.3	7.2	4.9
1821–30	8.9	1.5	1.9	2.6	7.0	4.4
1831–40	9.6	1.4	3.0	2.4	6.6	4.2
1841–50	10.4	1.4	5.3	1.4	5.1	3.7
1851–60	9.0	1.2	3.9	1.5	5.1	3.6

Notes: the estimates of GNP used by Feinstein and Crafts converge after 1830. After that date Feinstein's revised figures for gross domestic fixed capital formation can therefore be related to the GDP series that he used in his original calculations (table 4.1). Before 1830 the constant price GDP series that he originally used can be recalculated to conform to Crafts's views. Crafts accepts Feinstein's capital formation figures (*British economic growth*, p. 72). It is therefore possible to construct his implied GDP totals from the differences in investment percentages recorded in table 4.1. For example, Feinstein's investment percentage for 1811–20 is 11.3 (the figures in table 4.1 were rounded: for these calculations I have expressed the percentages more exactly). Crafts's estimates may be taken as (8.5 + 11.2)/2 = 9.85. Feinstein used a GDP estimate for the decade of £200m. Therefore Crafts implied estimate is £200m × (11.3/9.85) = £229m. Values for 1770 and 1790 in Craft's series in table 4.1 were obtained by interpolation. Once the revised GDP series has been established, the percentages shown in the above table may be calculated directly.
Sources: Feinstein, 'Capital formation in Great Britain', tab. 28, p. 91; idem, 'National totals, 1750–1920'; Crafts, *British economic growth*, tab. 4.1, p. 73.

ces relate only to the trend in GNP. The results are set out in table 4.3, and the detailed steps involved in deriving the estimates are described in the notes to the table.

Re-expressed in this fashion other features of investment over the century 1761–1860 emerge. For example, the stability of investment in agriculture as a percentage of GDP over the first six decades of the period covered by the table is striking, varying between a minimum of 1.9 per cent and a maximum of 2.0 per cent. Thereafter the percentage of GDP devoted to agricultural investment fell over the next four decades, but only modestly, to a little under two-thirds of its earlier level. The investment percentage devoted to mineral-related aspects of the economy was low and stable before 1800, then rose moderately during the first two decades of the nineteenth century and very sharply in the 1830s and 1840s to a peak of 5.3 per cent in the 1840s, when it was more than five times as high as it had been in the first decade of the century.

All exercises of this type are subject to very substantial margins of error.[14] It may be hazardous, for example, even to assume a stable percentage level of investment in agriculture over the period 1761–1820, as the data in table 4.3 suggest. On the other hand, it is quite possible that the apparent stability extended over a much longer period of development within the advanced organic economy. Crafts suggests a figure of 4.0 per cent for gross domestic investment as a proportion of GNP in 1700, compared with 6.0 per cent in 1760.[15] At first blush this suggests that the percentage share of agriculture must have been substantially lower at the earlier than at the later date, even allowing for the possibility that it was a larger fraction of total investment in 1700. However, it is worth remarking that investment in residential dwellings, which comprised another major claim on investment at the time (see row 3 of the upper panel of table

[14] As Feinstein strongly emphasized in discussing capital accumulation and economic growth: 'As will be painfully clear to anyone who has studied the preceding pages, there have been very few items for which precise, objective, and comprehensive data could be found: we have hardly any records of actual expenditure or statistics of the number of assets of a particular type constructed or in place. In almost every case we have had to rely on fragmentary evidence held together by a multitude of more or less arbitrary assumptions.' Feinstein, 'Capital formation in Great Britain', p. 82.

[15] Crafts, British economic growth, tab. 4.1, p. 73.

4.2), was probably at a very much lower level early in the century because population was virtually stationary then, the depreciation of capital in the form of housing is very slow and the rate of growth of population has a marked leverage on estimates of investment in residential dwellings, using the approach adopted by Feinstein.[16] At all events table 4.3 may be said to lend credence to the argument that the organic economy displayed a capacity for growth but not for acceleration, and that it was the grafting on to this base of a new vehicle for growth, possessing very different characteristics, that lifted the level of investment and the overall growth rate to an unprecedented level.[17] It is certainly worthy of remark that if investment related to the mineral-based energy economy is excluded from calculations of the percentage of GDP devoted to gross domestic fixed capital investment (table 4.3, column 5), there is no secular rise in investment in England over the century covered by the table, and if investment in residential dwellings is also excluded (table 4.3, column 6), since it was much influenced by demographic factors, there is no great change over time of any sort apart from an unusually high figure in 1811–20 and two low figures in the two final decades.

Concentration on aggregate measures of capital investment, therefore, suggesting a relatively smooth acceleration, may predispose the unwary to regard as a unitary and progressive phenomenon something which was the result of two different growth paths with contrasting characteristics. Forms of growth that had always tended to be plagued by negative feedback existed concurrently with new forms of growth characterized by positive feedback stemming from a new productive base. The former continued much as before during the century beginning in 1760; the latter provided a new dimension to growth and some exceptional opportunities for investment.

[16] Feinstein, 'Capital formation in Great Britain', pp. 42–3.
[17] As Deane remarked, 'in the British industrial revolution the process of transition from a pre-industrial growth path to a modern growth path depended not so much on expanding the national rate of savings or investment as on diverting investment from traditional to modern forms of capital accumulation'. Deane, 'Capital in the industrial revolution', p. 359.

Change: a unitary process?

Associated with the investigation of the shift from the advanced organic mode of production to the mineral-based energy economy is the question of whether the transition to the latter was implicit in the nature of the earlier system. If so, the nature of the connection needs to be specified. If not, the supposition that the entire process of change and growth from Tudor to Victorian times is in some sense unitary is further called in question. The relative importance of continuity and chance is an issue that must be faced.

The example of Holland is once more instructive. Holland achieved an exceptional success within the canons of an organic economy at a very early date. As in the case of England a century later, success entailed a demand for better transport and for the deployment of much larger quantities of energy within the productive system. The topography and hydrography of Holland offered the opportunity to solve the first problem. The creation of a passenger canal network during the first half of the seventeenth century showed that Holland possessed the enterprise, capital and technical and organizational skills needed to seize the opportunity.[18] Moreover, Dutch peat provided for a time a source of heat energy, if not mechanical energy, commensurate with the economic opportunities of the time, thus making possible a brief flowering of Dutch industrial supremacy in textiles, shipbuilding, brewing and sugar refining. But, though peat could briefly support vigorous expansion, it could not sustain a prolonged burst of growth.

As a source of energy capital the Dutch peat deposits fell part way between the use of virgin timber stands on the one hand and the opening up of a major coalfield on the other in the size of the stock of energy available, and therefore the scale and duration of the boost to economic growth that they could sustain. An unexploited forest area may provide, say, the charcoal needed for a flourishing iron industry for a few decades, after which the industry must either move on elsewhere, or, if it remains, content itself with turning into charcoal whatever annual volume of wood consumption is consonant with a sustained yield basis of exploitation, which, by definition, means an

[18] De Vries, 'Barges and capitalism'.

end to growth. Large peat deposits may allow a more substantial expansion over perhaps a century, but, though the period of growth may be longer, the subsequent contraction must be more painful since energy sources that take the form of a stock rather than a flow cannot be put on a sustained yield basis. With coal the time scale stretches out to several centuries. Individual mines become exhausted, of course, but large coalfield areas contain stores of energy that utterly dwarf those to be found in forests or peat beds, and the higher combustion temperatures of coal enable it to be used in processes for which wood or peat cannot be used, or can be used only far less effectively.[19]

Gaining access to deeper coal measures presented severe problems as drainage and haulage difficulties increased, but the consciousness that great riches were available as a tangible reward for success provided a very powerful incentive to the ingenious and persistent. The exhaustion of peat beds, preceded by rising extraction costs, presented different problems. Digging deeper was no solution. English or Scottish coal could be imported but its price to the final consumer in Holland was higher than in more favoured locations in Britain, leaving Dutch industry in a difficult competitive situation.[20] Dutch industries dependent upon cheap heat energy tended to stagnate or decline.

An economy may seize upon a cheap source of energy, exploit it with vigour, develop industries that require heat on a large scale to produce competitively, and yet find itself powerless to prevent their subsequent decline if the energy is drawn from an energy stock rather than an energy flow and the stock becomes exhausted. The existence of a clear need does not imply that the need will be met.

Inasmuch as the growth taking place in some sectors of the English economy was contingent upon the use of cheap energy on a large scale and that energy came from coal, it seems prudent to regard such growth not as a structural feature logically comparable to the benefits derived from specialization of function, or from the

[19] It is interesting to note that Isaac and John Wilkinson experimented with the use of peat as a fuel to smelt haemetite ore in their Cartmel furnace, before falling back on the use of charcoal. John later moved to the Black Country and succeeded in using coal for smelting: Lord, *Capital and steam power*, p. 27.

[20] Unger, 'Energy sources for the Dutch golden age', pp. 242–8.

development of the landlord, tenant farmer and labourer system in agriculture, but as an uncovenanted blessing. To describe this blessing as the gift of chance rather than the offspring of continuous development may seem an exercise in hyperbole. Coal production grew gradually and continuously over a long period, but in the sense that the presence of a relative abundance of coal in accessible seams is a rare geological feature, unconnected with other resources or with the prevailing economic system; and that the absence of abundant and accessible coal, or an equivalent capital stock of energy, meant that there was no escape from the logical constraints of an organic economy, no matter how successful the economy might be within such bounds, it may not be too great a liberty with language to refer to chance. To succeed in breaking free from the limitations experienced by all organic economies, a country needed not only to be capitalist in the conventional sense, to have become modernized, but also to be capitalist in the sense that its raw materials were drawn increasingly from mineral stocks rather than from the annual flow of agricultural production, and, above all, in the sense that it could tap great stores of energy rather than depend upon the kinds of renewable energy sources that had always previously provided any heat or power needed for production. The English economy was capitalist in both senses of the word, but the connection between the two was initially casual rather than causal.

The eighteenth and nineteenth centuries reconsidered

Viewed in this way the later eighteenth and early nineteenth centuries appear in a different light. The period emerges as a time of uncertainty when the rising difficulties inherent in organic economies towards the end of a phase of growth threatened to arrest further progress, but were matched by the rising opportunities brought into being by the switch to a mineral-based energy economy. The uncertainty is reflected in the behaviour of the key defining indicator of an industrial revolution. Real income per head had been rising between the mid-seventeenth and mid-eighteenth centuries because of the benefits which flowed from an increasingly efficient organic economy, not squandered in over-rapid population growth. For the next century its path was uncertain overall. For those workers most firmly rooted in an organic economy, notably the wage earners in the agricultural south and east, the dominant movement was probably downwards. For those increasingly affected by the creation of a new mode of economic life, however, situated chiefly in the industrial north, there may have been advance, though the local situation was often complicated by the slow decline of domestic industry, sometimes in the most miserable circumstances.

Until almost the middle of the nineteenth century it was still reasonable to fear a fate for England similar to that which had overtaken Holland. Hence the prominence of the stationary state in the prognostications of the classical economists. As the elements in the economy whose growth implied no increased pressure on the land gradually expanded, however, such forebodings lost their dread. Compositional change was slowly increasing the proportion of the workforce in occupations with high or rising productivity while technical change was improving productivity even in some of the most traditional trades. Even activities in which specialization of function could hold out little hope of enhanced productivity because the product was not standardized could benefit eventually from the discovery of ways of harnessing the new materials and energy sources in the production process. A seamstress with an electric sewing machine can produce a ball dress considerably quicker than a seamstress with a needle.

The favourable economic developments were paralleled by helpful demographic changes. Population growth rates receded somewhat from the high water mark set early in the nineteenth century and never returned to that peak. The advent of a steady upward trend in real incomes in the third and fourth quarters of the century, so far from provoking a resurgence in growth rates, and in spite of the rapid fall in mortality after 1870, ushered in a period of revolutionary fertility change without earlier precedent. Marital fertility fell so far and so fast that population increase slowly ebbed towards a zero or negative intrinsic growth rate. In this respect, if in no other, the expectations of the classical economists concerning the stationary state were fulfilled.

It is in keeping with the dual nature of the long period of economic growth culminating in the industrial revolution that some attributes of change should be closely related to each other, while others were not. For example, Adam Smith catalogued a series of political, legal, constitutional and social structural features that were conducive to the type of economic progress analysed in the *Wealth of nations*. Allowing for differences in terminology they are similar to the changes specified in modernization theory, as we have already noted, and are inter-related. Other attributes which Adam Smith did not mention could be added to the list. For example, the very high mobility of the English population, itself closely related to the institution of service and the peculiarities of the English marriage system,[21] made for a flexible response to economic opportunity, while the responsiveness of decisions to marry to prevailing economic circumstances was of crucial importance to preserving a favourable balance between production and reproduction.[22] These were all attributes that assisted in advancing the organic economy in England to an unusually high level of sophistication and achievement. As long as growth was taking place primarily within the context of an organic economy, the possession of this cluster of attributes was important in facilitating growth, and its absence a serious handicap. Many of the attributes of most importance, notably those relating to landholding and to marriage, were deeply rooted in the peculiarities of English society and were not capable of adoption abroad by conscious policy decisions, a fact which helps to explain the length of the period during which the English economy steadily strengthened in comparison to its continental rivals.

When the impetus to further growth began to be derived increasingly from the mineral-based energy sector of the economy, the same considerations no longer applied. The adoption of methods by which heat energy and mechanical energy could be harnessed on a vast scale in the production process, and the increasing substitution of mineral for organic raw materials, were developments which it proved easy to introduce from England into other socio-economic and political contexts. They represented sources of increased productivity that were footloose and exportable in contrast to the position

[21] See esp. Kussmaul, *Servants in husbandry*.

[22] For some recent reflections both on the available data about nuptiality and on their interpretation, see Smith, 'Fertility, economy and household formation'; Weir, 'Rather never than late'; Schofield 'English marriage patterns revisited'; and Goldstone, 'The demographic revolution in England'.

when the organic economy prevailed. Previously the institutional framework of growth had been more important than its material technology and therefore far less easy to transfer.

Thorstein Veblen was grappling with the same general issue when he wrote *Imperial Germany*.[23] It is also a matter that has helped to cause a confusion in Marxist thinking about social change and industrial development. If the sweep of English history during the centuries before and during the industrial revolution represents a unitary and progressive phenomenon it is natural to suppose that the later stages can only be reached after having first traversed the earlier stages. It is reasonable to expect, for example, that a bourgeois state should precede an industrial revolution. But, whereas it may be logical to expect this to be true in relation to the kind of economic growth that characterized the advanced organic economy, it is much less certain that the same should hold true in relation to the mineral-based energy economy. To the degree that the original association between the latter and its predecessor was a matter of coincidence rather than necessity in the land of its origin, its subsequent successful translation to other countries with very different social, political, legal and economic structures is not a matter for great surprise.

Individualism and welfare provision

It is in keeping with what might be termed the neutrality of the new sources of growth with respect to social and political context that many things should *not* have changed at the time of the gradual transfer to a mineral-based energy economy, or that they should have changed out of phase with the economic changes. It is evident that the chronology of demographic change bore little relation to that of the industrial revolution, certainly as it is normally understood. The same was also conspicuously true of familial structure, co-residential arrangements and kinship ties. The exercise in demographic and social structural research that exploded the myth that Juliet's early marriage was typical of any but the aristocracy in Tudor times also demonstrated that the small conjugal family had been the normal co-residential unit in England for many centuries,

[23] Veblen, *Imperial Germany*.

and that a statutory system of public provision for the widowed, orphaned, sick and even, in some circumstances, for the unemployed had transferred the burden of support for the disadvantaged and unfortunate from the resources of kin to the public purse.[24] This complex of social, familial and economic arrangements continued throughout the industrial revolution period without striking change. Indeed, it is in large measure fair to regard the welfare state, sometimes treated as the product of recent developments in views about communal responsibility for those least well able to look after themselves, as representing no more than the transfer to a centralized administrative system of responsibility for the discharge of a range of functions previously performed by the parish.

The question of the way in which help is extended to those unable to fend for themselves is a matter of profound importance in any society. It is a source of weakness in the historiography of the industrial revolution and of modernization theory that it is so widely misunderstood. Because the topic can easily acquire strong ideological overtones it is much subject to myth-making. Both apologists for capitalism and opponents of the capitalist system tend to assume that with its rise atomistic individualism became a reality, superseding an older world in which family and kin provided support for the orphaned, the elderly, the unemployed, the crippled, the sick and the mad. Traditional ties were dissolved; each man or woman was obliged to depend upon self where previously he or she could have turned to kin.[25] For one school this was a precondition for rapid economic growth, with the ultimate benefit far outweighing the individual sufferings that were engendered in the process. For the other the growth was bought at an appalling price in human suffering not adequately alleviated until the state began to siphon off some of the flow of new wealth from private pockets into the public purse,

[24] Laslett, *The world we have lost*; idem, 'The family and the collectivity'; and idem, 'The wrong way through the telescope'. The growth of knowledge since Laslett published the first edition of *The world we have lost* in 1965 has caused him to modify and expand his thesis (as in the third edition, 1983), but the central argument remains the same.

[25] This line of thought has been pursued in many contexts. See, for example, Macfarlane's discussion of the surge of witchcraft prosecutions in late sixteenth-century Essex in *Witchcraft in Tudor and Stuart England*.

and used the resources thus made available to lay the foundations of the welfare state.

Atomistic individualism was always a convenient abstraction, never a universal historical reality. In all periods of history a large proportion of all those living at a given point in time have been incapable of looking after themselves. No baby or small child can exist independently, and those who live to advanced years tend to become increasingly dependent on others as the years pass. At all ages, moreover, the accident of illness or economic misfortune may have the effect of temporarily incapacitating an individual and leaving him or her dependent for a while on the resources and goodwill of others. It might be nearer the truth to say that the development of capitalism in England was conditional upon the existence of an efficient and ubiquitous welfare system than to say that it could only flourish by undermining the old system of welfare provision. The system of support created by the old poor law covered much the same range of life-cycle hazards as are covered by the state today, sometimes on a relative scale uncannily similar to that current nowadays. For example, outrelief for the elderly in the eighteenth century, expressed as a fraction of the daily adult male wage, was not much different from the scale of old age pensions today, similarly expressed.[26]

The difference does not lie in the nature or scale of provision made but in the unit through which transfer payments are made; the state has replaced the parish. Viewed in this light the creation and elaboration of the poor law system from the reign of Elizabeth onwards was an important reason for the development of a capitalist system in England, affording the kind of provision for those in need which gave individuals a degree of protection against the hazards of life that in typical peasant cultures were provided by kin. Procreation and the rearing of children remained within the family and underwrote the continued central role of the conjugal family unit. The community did not attempt to encroach in this sphere, but other life-cycle dangers were met through parish provision, so that beyond childhood men and women could look to a source other than their kin to

[26] See Smith, 'Some issues concerning families'; Thomson, 'The decline of social welfare'; Wales, 'Poverty, poor relief and the life-cycle'; Newman Brown, 'The receipt of poor relief'.

assist when they could not provide for themselves. Such provision did not imply that kin were completely ignored and unimportant; nor was such provision always either sufficient or administered sympathetically. But it facilitated the growth of an economy where mobility was high, where contract could supplant custom, where the individual could risk losing intimate contact with kin. The obstacles to rapid economic development described by anthropologists familiar with Third World countries in the recent past were absent or much less prominent in early modern England because of the convenient symbiosis of a capitalist ethos in large tracts of economic life with the provision of the range of welfare services needed to enable the community to accommodate to its rigours without producing intolerable stresses amongst those whom the accidents of life or the imperfections of the system had rendered incapable of fending for themselves.[27]

Both the empirical and theoretical issues involved in this question are complex, and prohibit its full treatment in the compass of an essay, but, since the prevailing perception tends to be so different, it may be of interest to note that in a recent exercise in the casting up of early national income accounts, Stone has estimated that social welfare provision represented a fifth of the combined total of central and local government expenditure in the late seventeenth century, if Gregory King's data are put into a modern national income accounting framework.[28] It is also instructive that Petty, often depicted as representative of the new age and its attitudes, in discussing the heads under which government spending could most conveniently be broken down, named the care of the poor and measures to alleviate unemployment as the only categories of expenditure which it was desirable to increase.[29] All others, including defence, he

[27] Although his treatment of English history is unsatisfactory, Hagen conveyed effectively the inadequacy of purely economic analyses of the problems of inducing growth in the Third World in the immediately post-war decades in *Theory of social change*. His arguments are the more persuasive in that he wrote as an economist.

[28] Stone, *Some British empiricists* (in the chapter on Gregory King).

[29] Stone summarized Petty's division of public expenditure into six 'branches of the publick charge' as falling into the following categories: foreign war and civil strife; the 'Governours' – the king, his ministers and civil servants; the church; education; the care of the poor; and measures to alleviate unemployment. Stone, *Some British empiricists*. Petty's views are set out in *Treatise of taxes and contributions*, pp. 18–31. In his own words, 'We enumerated six branches of the publick charge, and have slightly spoken how four of them might be lessened; we come next to two branches, whereof we shall rather recommend the augmentation.'

wished to see reduced if possible. The ability of the individual to look after himself is paradoxically intimately bound up with his ability to draw upon a larger pool of resources in a range of circumstances that are widely agreed to constitute proper grounds for communal help.[30]

Topics to explore

Numbers and notions form the dialectic of economic and demographic history. It is a matter of good fortune for them that quantitative material should figure prominently in their output, not because quantified material has an objective validity denied to other types of evidence, nor because numbers confer precision. Insofar as they appear to do so, the apparent precision is frequently spurious. The value of quantitative data lies chiefly in the help they may afford in distinguishing between notions that should continue to stand and those that should fall. Decisive advance in any subject is a matter of better ideas, more satisfactory models, more elegant concepts, but distinguishing between alternative theories is seldom easy and the assistance of numbers may be of great value in this regard. In considering the soundness of Malthus's model of the functioning of an organic economy, for example, it was of great value to be able to move from the observation that in principle fertility changes induced by nuptiality shifts *could* be of decisive importance in determining population growth to the demonstration that they *were* so.[31] Similarly, it is one thing to hypothesize that population growth rates and trends in the prices of the necessaries of life should be closely related, because, say, of the operation of the principle of declining marginal returns, but another to be able to show a close and consistent relationship between the rates of change in the two variables.[32]

Usually, the interplay of numbers and notions begins with the formulation of a testable hypothesis, moves to the assemblage of relevant data and later involves the employment of appropriate sta-

[30] The great debating point in this regard from the sixteenth to the twentieth centuries has been the extent of community responsibility for what the Elizabethans called 'sturdy beggars' – those who were well able to work but either unable or unwilling to find work. Distinguishing between the unable and the unwilling has never been easy.

[31] The key data are set out in Wrigley, 'The growth of population in eighteenth-century England', fig. 5, p. 141. See also Wrigley and Schofield, *Population history of England*, pp. 421–35.

[32] See fig. 2.1, p. 63.

tistical methods to establish the strength, direction and consistency of any relationship between the variables concerned. Sometimes, however, the sequence is reversed because the prior assemblage of quantitative data brings to light the existence of a relationship which virtually requires an attempt to formulate hypotheses that can make sense of what has been observed. The dialectic is initiated from empirical observation rather than from the construction of a model of reality. For example, there was a quite remarkably close relationship over a period of at least three centuries in England between changes in general fertility and those in illegitimate fertility, a relationship whose character and consistency was entirely unexpected when it was first demonstrated. When marriage was late, celibacy high and general fertility in consequence low, the illegitimacy ratio was also low, even though the number of unmarried women was, of course, very high as a proportion of all women of child-bearing age. Equally, when there were few women of child-bearing age unmarried, and overall fertility was in consequence high, the illegitimacy ratio was nonetheless always high.[33] The illegitimacy *rate*, for obvious reasons, must have fluctuated even more strikingly.[34] The observed relationship runs against expectation, since, *ceteris paribus*, it might be expected that the fact of a high proportion of women living outside marriage but in the reproductive age groups would result in a larger number of illegitimate births than when the proportion was low. The discovery of a persistent, if perverse, pattern of this sort continuing for many centuries in England is especially intriguing in that in France, for example, the 'expected' relationship appears to have existed.[35] The facts represent a challenge to those with a taste for theorizing.

Turning in the same spirit to the history of the industrial revolution, a number of topics come to mind where the dialectic between notions and numbers may prove fruitful in future research.

The first concerns energy usage. The existence of a strong link between income per head and energy consumption per head is a commonplace of economic analysis of the twentieth-century

[33] Wrigley, 'Marriage, fertility and population growth', pp. 167–82.
[34] For some perceptive comments on the illegitimacy ratio and illegitimacy rates, see Drake. 'Norway', pp. 299–307.
[35] See Wrigley, 'Marriage, fertility and population growth'.

world.[36] It is plausible to suppose that in the past, when energy was much scarcer, the relationship may have been even stronger. There are persuasive general reasons for expecting to find such a link, but the subject has not so far been widely investigated.[37]

Although the most spectacular changes in the quantity of mechanical energy available per worker occurred in the wake of the development of the steam engine as a vehicle for converting the vast quantities of heat available in coal into mechanical work, there had previously been wide differences between organic economies in the scale of mechanical energy that the average worker disposed of. Agricultural systems in which draught animals were plentiful could presumably achieve substantially higher labour productivity than those where horses and oxen were scarce. A man has at best about a tenth of the power output of a horse.[38] Thus, where fodder was plentiful and animal power therefore relatively cheap, the carriage of goods overland could be comparatively inexpensive. The same was true in relation to mine drainage, the winding of minerals to the surface and mineral transport both above and below ground. And many industrial processes could be carried out more quickly, on a larger scale and more cheaply where horse power could be used freely as the prime mover. Bizarre accidents sometimes brought home the importance of animal power in a vivid and painful fashion. One major reason why the convict settlement in New South Wales for so long disappointed the home government in its expectation that the colony would rapidly achieve self-sufficiency in food was that

[36] As Cipolla remarked, 'It is rather important to realize that high per capita consumption of energy not only means more energy for consumption, heating, lighting, household appliances, cars, etc., but also means more energy for production, i.e. more energy available per worker and therefore higher productivity of labour.' *Economic history of world population*, p. 52.

[37] The evidence of the recent past, though no doubt it rests on shaky empirical foundations, suggests that the relationship between energy use and output per head is curvilinear, with small increases in energy usage being associated with large percentage rises in productivity when usage is low. When energy usage is high, further productivity gains require large percentage increases in energy consumption. Kindleberger, *Economic development*, fig. 4.4, p. 70.

[38] Levasseur assumed that one horse power equalled that of twenty-one men (p. 76 above). Other calculations yield results suggesting that one horse power is equivalent to between ten and thirty manpower. Ubbelohde, *Man and energy*, p. 62.

draught animals proved hard to keep alive during the tediously long passage to Australia, nor was London responsive to requests for more shipments of such livestock. As a result for a generation there was reversion to hoe agriculture.[39]

Energy in the form of heat was also important. Once again there was great variation in availability between different organic economies as well as between them as a group and economies using mineral sources of energy. At one extreme sufferings like those of the rural poor in Bangladesh today, for which there are many historical parallels, arise in part from a combination of the necessity of expending a modest amount of heat energy to make food edible with the high price of even the most ineffective of fuels.[40] At the other extreme, areas of new settlement sometimes possessed a great wealth of standing timber and could enjoy for a time a profligate use of heat energy at a comparatively trivial cost. As late as the 1870s, when her population already exceeded 40 million and industrialization was advancing fast, half the total energy requirements of the United States were still met from wood.[41] England's good fortune in possessing and exploiting a plentiful new source of heat energy lay at the root of contrasts that began to be noted by eighteenth-century travellers. Arthur Young, for example, was struck by the fact that in the windows of a large village in the Garonne valley he was unable to see even a single pane of glass.[42] Cheap and abundant heat is needed to produce glass on any scale, and glass must therefore remain a luxury wherever organic materials are the sole source of heat.

Information about energy production and usage in the past is far less complete and detailed than one might wish, but experimental

[39] Very little cultivation by plough was undertaken until after 1805, and carts were rarely used for transport. In the early years of settlement corn was cut by sickle and taken to store on men's backs. Dunsdorfs, *Australian wheat-growing industry*, pp. 11–14; Coghlan, *Labour and industry in Australia*, I, pp. 114–16. Phillip, the first governor, was relatively successful in getting cattle to New South Wales, but within a few months of landing, the small herd was lost in mysterious circumstances, to be rediscovered several years later in 1795, grown to about sixty head. Ibid., p. 118; Tench, *Expedition to Botany Bay*, p. 61.

[40] See above p. 53.

[41] And a further fifth of energy needs was met by the fodder consumed by draught animals. Coal still ranked only third. Fisher, *Energy crises*, fig. 2.1, p. 14.

[42] Young, *Travels in France*, p. 29; see also pp. 21, 27, 211.

calculations soon show that the energy potential of the different possible sources of heat and mechanical energy differed so greatly that even order of magnitude estimates of the output from each major energy source may reveal very large contrasts over time in the same country, or between countries. Assembling such estimates, and perhaps estimates of the use made of the energy produced, should prove feasible for England from, say, Tudor times onwards, and perhaps for some other west European countries or regions, and any relationship between energy production and use and major economic indicators might then be clarified.

A second topic that might repay investigation is the effect of specialization of function on productivity and the associated question of occupational structure. The parable of the pinmakers has had a very powerful influence over almost all subsequent writing about the growth in output per head. The details of the parable prove far from persuasive upon investigation. Adam Smith wrote that the making of a pin could be broken down into eighteen distinct operations, and claimed that he had seen a small manufactory in which only ten men were employed. Hence the full possibilities of subdivision of function had not been realized and some men were performing two or three different operations. Nevertheless they could 'when they exerted themselves' make about 12 pounds of pins a day. Each pound contained upwards of 4,000 pins, so that the 10 men between them could make at least 48,000 pins a day. A little arithmetic suggests doubt about Adam Smith's claim. Each pin's manufacture is said to have involved eighteen distinct operations, which implies a total of 864,000 distinct operations in the course of a day's work. Assuming each man worked for 10 hours unremittingly, he would have had to perform 2.4 distinct operations each second throughout the day to have enabled a total of 48,000 pins to be manufactured. This would involve a degree of dexterity and assiduity that seems implausible. Adam Smith probably also exaggerated the low productivity of the isolated worker, which he asserted might be so low as to prevent him even completing 1 pin in a day's work, and would certainly prohibit him from turning out 20.[43]

In spite of the unwarranted overstatement of the rise in productivity among the pinmakers arising from specialization of function,

[43] Smith, *Wealth of nations*, ed. Cannan, I, p. 9.

there can no doubt that the potential gains were very substantial. To estimate the impact of any enhanced productivity achieved in this way on the level of output per head generally, and hence on the scope for improving real incomes, however, it is necessary not only to quantify the extent of the gain in output per worker in the industry affected, but also the fraction of the total labour force working in the industry. Neither calculation is easy to carry out for lack of relevant data, but the significance of the issue suggests that a determined attempt should be made. In particular, it would be especially illuminating to uncover evidence bearing on the question whether the available gains, though substantial, were also limited, in the sense that output per head ceased to rise when market size increased beyond some threshold level.

Adam Smith himself suggested that this was so in pin manufacture, by implication at least. When he mentioned that there were only ten men in the manufactory that he visited but that eighteen distinct operations were carried out, he implied that even the very high output per man which he reported could be increased in a plant with a larger workforce. But he also implied that there would be an upper limit to the productivity per man attainable if the process as a whole was broken down into a maximum of eighteen specialist tasks. To achieve maximum levels of productivity might clearly involve employing more than eighteen men, since the time necessary to perform each discrete operation would naturally vary, so that, for example, it might require four men pointing the wire for each man cutting it into strips, and so on; but it is a reasonable inference from his discussion of the issue that whereas the output of ten men would be vastly higher per man than that of a single worker, and the output of fifty men higher per man than that of ten, though in a much reduced degree, the output of a hundred men would be no greater per man than that of fifty, or would differ only negligibly. Convincing evidence on this matter has a bearing on the question of the general secular growth possibilities in this mode compared with those associated with the increased use of power per worker.[44]

[44] This discussion of the specialization issue is, of course, no more than a sketch, some might say a caricature. In particular, the introduction of machinery to enhance productivity greatly complicates matters. It may well mark a stage in increasing specialization and be regarded as a concomitant of it, and it may substantially raise output per man. In the absence of cheap mechanical energy on a large scale, however, the scale of the boost to productivity is apt to be limited, and the range of operable machines restricted.

The second element in the attempt to quantify the significance of specialization of function is of as great, if not greater, importance. If Adam Smith's parable had been widely applicable, industrial revolutions would have been events worthy only of slight remark. Any country that *failed* to experience one would have attracted far more attention. An increase in productivity per head far less striking than that in his parable would have sufficed without difficulty if, say, half the workforce had participated in the change. Patently this was not the case. Indeed, it is obvious that if he was correct about the order of magnitude of improvement in productivity attainable, only a modest fraction of the labour force would have needed to be affected to have produced a massive change in the economy as a whole. Adam Smith talked of a *minimum* rise in output per head within the pinmaking industry of 240-fold as a result of specialization. We have already noted that this was almost certainly a gross exaggeration, but, had it been correct, it would imply that if only 5 per cent of the labour force underwent such a revolutionary change in productivity, while the remaining 95 per cent remained unaffected, aggregate output, and average output per head, would both have risen thirteen-fold, assuming that output per head in the 5 per cent concerned had previously been close to the national average, though, of course, the effect on the value of the aggregate output would have been less pronounced, given the effects on the price of commodities likely to follow from such large changes in their supply.

I have already drawn attention to the data published in the 1831 census that makes it possible to quantify for that date the comparatively small fraction of the adult male labour force that was employed either in industries whose productivity might have been increased by specialization of function or in industries where productivity was rising because of the increasing use of mechanical energy derived from coal;[45] but far more work is needed. In due course it should be possible to narrow the wide margins of uncertainty that at present cloud discussion of the proportion of the labour force employed in industries with rising productivity per head, and show how that proportion changed over time. It is no less important to try to establish whether in forms of employment where the market was local, the opportunity for specialization slight or non-existent and production methods largely unaltered between Tudor and Georgian

[45] See above, p. 83–6.

times it is proper to assume that output per head had scarcely changed. These were activities which still employed a very large proportion of the workforce until the middle decades of the nineteenth century. Trades such as those of tailors, shoemakers, carpenters, masons and butchers weighed so heavily on the scales that even small changes in productivity in these occupations would have exerted a greater influence on overall productivity than any but the most spectacular changes in productivity among forms of employment like pinmaking. Clearly, too, unambiguous evidence of unchanging productivity in such employments would be of the highest value in assessing the wider significance of the changes occurring in industries, such as agriculture and shipping, for example, in which there can be no reasonable doubt that output per head rose progressively and substantially from late Tudor times onwards.[46]

Finally, to round off the inter-related questions of changes in output per head and changes in occupational structure, there would be value in obtaining fuller information about the overall picture for a different reason. We have seen that throughout the early modern period growth in England was notably unbalanced when compared with continental Europe, with far more pronounced changes in the percentages of the workforce engaged in different employment sectors than in, say, France.[47] Even with unchanging productivity per head in each sector, major alterations in the sectoral balance may imply significant overall change, if the movement is chiefly from low to high productivity sectors. Output per head in the coalmining industry, for example, does not appear to have undergone great change, but the number of men who dervied all or most of their income from work in the pits rose in step with the rise in coal output, which multiplied many times over between the accession of Elizabeth and the death of George III. Furthermore, in this case, even though productivity in coalmining may not have changed much, productivity in the transport activities closely associated with it probably grew substantially under the stimulus of the rapid increases in tonnages mined. The east coast shipping industry shared in the general rise of productivity in shipping; and there were also

---

[46] On agriculture see Wrigley, 'Urban growth and agricultural change'. The relevant literature on shipping has recently been surveyed by Ville, 'Total factor productivity in the English shipping industry'.

[47] See above pp. 12–17.

linked changes in the productivity per head of those who made their living from moving the coal while it was still on land. The metal railway and the flanged wheel transformed the productivity of man and horse alike in moving coal from the pithead to the coal staithe.[48]

Conclusion

The connecting thread running between all the types of empirical investigation just described is the desire to try to identify the sources of increased output per head, in the belief that increased output per head was the proximate cause of rising real incomes, which, in turn, if sufficiently substantial and sustained, provided the defining characteristic of an industrial revolution. Better information in this regard would be of the highest value, and might prove decisive in testing the validity of the basic thesis of this book – that two very different modes of economic growth each contributed to the trans- formation of England from a rural, agricultural, sparsely populated, poor and relatively backward economy in the sixteenth century into the first instance of a society capable of producing in such abundance that chronic poverty ceased to be an inescapable part of the human lot. The conventional categories of economic analysis do not easily distinguish the two modes, and most of the high-level theorizing about the transformation has emphasized its unitary nature. By deliberately taking liberties with the conventional usage of terms such as 'capitalist', and by laying emphasis on the conclusions drawn by contemporaries about the probable upshot of the economic trends of the time, I have sought to bring home the strin- gent limitations to growth that attended all economies, however capitalist (in the conventional sense) their structure, that were organic in their material base. I have described the features of the new mode of growth that was free from the old constraints (though not, of course, without grave perils of its own). And I have raised the question of the nature of the connection between the two modes, suggesting that it is better described as casual and coincidental than causal and inevitable.

[48] Flinn, *British coal industry*, pp. 146–53. Nef quotes an estimate that wagonways consisting of wooden rails enabled the horse or ox and his driver to move five to eight times as much coal from the pits to the water as had previously been possible: Nef, *British coal industry*, I, p. 385.

In relation to broad issues of interpretation, empirical evidence is seldom decisive. Old paradigms do not lose their currency overnight. But the advent of new ideas may cause an existing stock of empirical knowledge to be re-examined, and may serve to suggest what new work is most urgently needed. Work on the industrial revolution stands in need of a rejuvenating influence. The ideas advanced here will have served their purpose if they have such an effect.[49]

Looking back on the changes of the eighteenth and nineteenth centuries, a later generation lighted upon the term industrial revolution to describe them.[50] I remarked at the beginning of this work that the term industrial revolution was an unhappy conjunction of adjective and noun. It may be evidence of its unhandy nature that it has been used so little by some of those who have contributed most significantly to the study of the phenomenon whose character it is supposed to denote. Clapham, for example, provided separate indexes for each of the three large volumes of his *An economic history of modern Britain,* yet the term appears in the index only once, in the second volume, and then only in reference to a quotation from another author. Similarly, Deane and Cole, in what has probably been the most influential single work of economic history dealing with the transformation of Britain into an industrial state to be published since the Second World War, included the term in their index, but the entry again refers only to a single page and once more to the work of another author, Arnold Toynbee.[51] Such conspicuous neglect, and the catalogue could be lengthened, holds a lesson. Historians have found it very difficult to import a meaning to the term which was immediately useful to them in trying to communicate their ideas or information. This has been as true, perhaps more true, for those for whom the fact of the industrial revolution was the central feature of the intellectual landscape they surveyed as for those for whom the issue was more peripheral.

[49] 'True wisdom about the industrial revolution', McCloskey remarked, 'is that little is known, and much more can be known.' McCloskey, 'Industrial revolution', p.70.

[50] There is an intriguing, forcefully expressed review of the meanings attached to the term industrial revolution by economic historians over the past century in Cannadine, 'The present and the past in the English industrial revolution'.

[51] Deane and Cole, *British economic growth.*

The term itself may be too deeply embedded in general discourse to be uprooted, but if it is to regain the place in discussion that its intrinsic importance deserves, it needs to be invested with new attributes. In particular the tendency to assume that it was a unitary, progressive, integrated phenomenon has counted against its usefulness. While the identifying characteristic of an industrial revolution may helpfully be defined in simple terms as a substantial and progressive rise in real income per head, progress in understanding its nature, and its location in time and space, seems likely to depend upon a more explicit recognition that the immense changes taking place in the economy of England over the seventeenth, eighteenth and nineteenth centuries were the result of two modes of economic growth whose sources and secular prospects differed radically. Their joint effect is picked up in changing proportions by conventional measures of economic growth, but the fact that they blended in this fashion has helped to create an unfortunate and misleading illusion of uniformity of process.

In his inaugural lecture at Cambridge, Postan remarked that 'the penalty of being sufficiently concrete to be real is the impossibility of being sufficiently abstract to be exact'.[52] Tackling very large historical themes, like the genesis of the industrial revolution, involves even greater difficulties of this type than exist in other historical writing. A tension between clarity and comprehensiveness is inherent in all attempts to pay attention to both the wood and the trees. It is very tempting to try to keep matters simple; to avoid unnecessary complexity; to apply Occam's razor vigorously. But simplicity can be bought at too high a price; adding a character to the play may enable lines to be spoken without which the development of the plot is unintelligible. If I have yielded to the temptation to complicate a story already involved enough; if I have, indeed, to quote Postan again, indulged in 'the greatest of all joys, that of inventing new names',[53] it was done in the hope that it might help to revive interest in what was, in my view, the most important of all historical transformations to have taken place within these shores, the industrial revolution.

[52] Postan, 'The historical method in social science', p. 138.
[53] Ibid., pp. 129–30.

References

The following abbreviated forms of journal titles have been used in the list of references.

Afdeling Agrarische Geschiedenis Bijdragen	*A.A.G. Bijdragen*
Agricultural History Review	*Ag. Hist. Rev.*
Annales. Economies, Sociétés, Civilisations	*Annales, E.S.C.*
British Journal of Sociology	*Br. J. Soc.*
Business History	*Bus. Hist.*
Economic History Review	*Econ. Hist. Rev.*
English Historical Review	*Eng. Hist. Rev.*
Explorations in Economic History	*Explor. Econ. Hist.*
Historial Journal	*Hist. J.*
Journal of Economic History	*J. Econ. Hist.*
Journal of Family History	*J. Fam. Hist.*
Past and Present	*P. & P.*
Population and Development Review	*Pop. Dev. Rev.*
Population Studies	*Pop. Stud.*

Andorka, R., *Determinants of fertility in advanced societies* (London, 1978).

Ashton, T.S., *Iron and steel in the industrial revolution* (Manchester, 1924).

Baines, E., *History of cotton manufacture* (London, 1835).

Bairoch, P., 'Niveaux de développement économique de 1810 à 1910', *Annales, E.S.C.*, xx (1965), pp. 1091–117.

Becker, G.S., *A treatise on the family* (Cambridge, Mass., 1981).

Benaerts, P., *Les Origines de la grande industrie allemande* (Paris, 1933).

Botham, F.W. and Hunt, E.H., 'Wages in Britain during the industrial revolution', *Econ. Hist. Rev.*, 2nd ser., xl (1987), pp. 380–9.

Briscoe, J., 'Energy use and social structure in a Bangladesh village', *Pop. Dev. Rev.*, v (1979), pp. 615–41.

Bulatao, R.A. and Lee, R.D., eds., *Determinants of fertility in developing countries*, 2 vols. (New York, 1983).

Caldwell, J.C., *Theory of fertility decline* (London, 1982).

Cannandine, D., 'The present and the past in the English industrial revolution 1880–1980', *P. & P.*, cIII (1984), pp. 131–72.

Chandler, T. and Fox, G., *Three thousand years of urban growth* (New York, 1974).

Chesnais, J.-C., *La Transition démographique* (Paris, 1986).

Church, R., *The history of the British coal industry*, vol. III, *1830–1913: Victorian pre-eminence* (Oxford, 1986).

Cipolla, C., *The economic history of world population* (Harmondsworth, 1962).

Clapham, J.H., *An economic history of modern Britain*, 3 vols. (Cambridge, 1926–38).

Cleland, J. and Wilson, C., 'Demand theories of the fertility transition: an iconoclastic view', *Pop. Stud.*, xLI (1987), pp. 5–30.

Coghlan, T.A., *Labour and industry in Australia*, 4 vols. (Oxford, 1918).

Cole, J.W. and Wolf, E.R., *The hidden frontier: ecology and ethnicity in an Alpine valley* (New York, 1974).

Coleman, D.C., 'Proto-industrialization: a concept too many', *Econ. Hist. Rev.*, 2nd ser., xxxvi (1983), pp. 435–48.

Connell, K.H., *The population of Ireland, 1750–1845* (Oxford, 1950).

Cook, E., *Man, energy and society* (San Francisco, 1976).

Cottrell, F., *Energy and society: the relation between energy, social change, and economic development* (New York, 1955).

Crafts, N.F.R., 'British economic growth, 1700–1831: a review of the evidence', *Econ. Hist. Rev.*, 2nd ser., xxxvi (1983), pp. 177–99.
British economic growth during the industrial revolution (Oxford, 1985).

Deane, P., 'The role of capital in the industrial revolution', *Explor. Econ. Hist.*, x (1973), pp. 349–64.
The evolution of economic ideas (Cambridge, 1978).

Deane, P, and Cole, W.A., *British economic growth 1688–1959: trends and structure* (Cambridge, 1962).

de Vries, J., 'Barges and capitalism: passenger transportation in the Dutch economy, 1632–1839', *A.A.G. Bijdragen*, xxi (1978), pp. 33–398.
'Patterns of urbanization in pre-industrial Europe 1500–1800', in H. Schmal, ed., *Patterns of European urbanization since 1500* (London, 1981), pp. 79–109.
'The decline and rise of the Dutch economy, 1675–1900', *Research in Economic History*, supplement 3, *Essays in honor of William N. Parker* (1984), pp. 149–89.

European urbanization 1500–1800 (London, 1984).

de Zeeuw, J.W., 'Peat and the Dutch golden age: the historical meaning of energy attainability', *A.A.G. Bijdragen*, XXI (1978), pp. 3–31.

Drake, M., *Population and society in Norway 1735–1865* (Cambridge, 1969).

'Norway', in W.R. Lee, ed., *European demography and economic growth* (London, 1979), pp. 284–318.

Dunsdorfs, E., *The Australian wheat-growing industry 1788–1948* (Melbourne, 1956).

Easterlin, R.A., 'The economics and sociology of fertility: a synthesis', in C. Tilly, ed., *Historical studies of changing fertility* (Princeton, 1978), pp. 57–133.

Emery, F., 'Wales', in J. Thirsk, ed., *The agrarian history of England and Wales*, vol. v, pt I (Cambridge, 1984), pp. 393–428.

Feinstein, C.H., 'Capital formation in Great Britain', in P. Mathias and M.M. Postan, eds., *The Cambridge economic history of Europe* vol. VII, pt I (Cambridge, 1978), pp. 28–96.

'Part II, national totals, 1750–1920', in S. Pollard and C.H. Feinstein, eds., *Studies in capital formation in the United Kingdom, 1750–1920* (Oxford, 1988).

Fisher, J.C., *Energy crises in perspective* (New York, 1974).

Flinn, M.W., 'Trends in real wages, 1750–1850', *Econ. Hist. Rev.*, 2nd ser., XXVII (1974), pp. 395–413.

The history of the British coal industry, vol. II, *1700–1830: the industrial revolution* (Oxford, 1984).

Geertz, C., *Agricultural involution: the process of ecological change in Indonesia* (Berkeley, 1963).

Peddlers and princes: social change and economic modernization in two Indonesian towns (Chicago, 1963).

Goldstone, J.A., 'The demographic revolution in England: a re-examination', *Pop. Stud.*, XL (1986), pp. 5–33.

Grigg, D., *The dynamics of agricultural change: the historical experience* (London, 1982).

Hagen, E.E., *On the theory of social change: how economic growth begins* (London, 1964).

Hajnal, J., 'European marriage patterns in perspective', in D.V. Glass and D.E.C. Eversley, eds., *Population in history* (London, 1965), pp. 101–43.

'Two kinds of pre-industrial household formation systems', in R. Wall, ed., *Family forms in historic Europe* (Cambridge, 1983), pp. 65–104.

Hall, C.W., 'The role of energy in world agriculture and food availability', in D. Pimentel and C.W. Hall, eds., *Food and energy resources* (London, 1984), pp. 43–66.

Harris, J.R., 'Industry and technology in the eighteenth century: Britain and France', inaug. lecture (Birmingham, 1972).

Hills, R.L., *Power in the industrial revolution* (Manchester, 1970).

Himmelfarb, G., *The idea of poverty: England in the early industrial age* (London, 1984).

Houston, R.A. and Snell, K.D.M., 'Proto-industrialization? Cottage industry, social change, and industrial revolution', *Hist. J.*, XXVII (1984), pp. 473–92.

Hunt, E.H., 'Industrialization and regional inequality: wages in Britain, 1760–1914', *J. Econ. Hist.*, XLVI (1986), pp. 935–66.

Jackson, R.V., 'Growth and deceleration in English agriculture, 1660–1790', *Econ. Hist. Rev.*, 2nd ser., XXXVIII (1985), pp. 333–51.

Jacquemyns, G., *Histoire de la crise économique des Flandres (1845–50)*, Académie Royale de Belgique. Classe des lettres et des sciences morales et politiques. Mémoires, deuxième série, XVIII (Brussels, 1929), pp. 1–472.

Kindleberger, C.P., *Economic development*, 2nd edn (New York, 1965).

King, G., 'The LCC Burns Journal', a manuscript notebook containing workings for several projected works (composed c. 1695–1700), in *The earliest classics: John Graunt and Gregory King*, introd. P. Laslett (1973).

Kussmaul, A., *Servants in husbandry in early modern England* (Cambridge, 1981).

Landes, D.C., 'Technological change and development in western Europe, 1750–1914', in H.J. Habbakuk and M. Postan, eds., *The Cambridge economic history of Europe*, vol. VI, pt I (Cambridge, 1965), pp. 274–601.

Langdon, J., 'The economics of horses and oxen in medieval England', *Ag. Hist. Rev.*, XXX (1982), pp. 31–40.

'Horse hauling: a revolution in vehicle transport in twelfth- and thirteenth-century England?', *P. & P.*, CIII (1984), pp. 37–66.

Laslett, P., *The world we have lost* (London, 1965).

'The wrong way through the telescope: a note on literary evidence in sociology and in historical sociology', *Br. J. Soc.*, XXVII (1976), pp. 319–42.

'Characteristics of the western family considered over time', *J. Fam. Hist.*, II (1977), pp. 89–115.

'The family and the collectivity', *Sociology and Social Research*, LXIII (1979), pp. 432–42.

Levasseur, E., *La Population française*, 3 vols. (Paris, 1889–92).

Levine, D., *Family formation in an age of nascent capitalism* (New York, 1977).

Lewis, W.A., *The theory of economic growth* (London, 1955).

Lindert, P.H. and Williamson, J.G., 'English workers' living standards during the industrial revolution: a new look', *Econ. Hist. Rev.*, 2nd ser., xxxvi (1983), pp. 1–25.

Lord, J., *Capital and steam power 1750–1800*, introd. W.H. Chaloner, 2nd edn (London, 1966).

McCloskey, D., 'The industrial revolution 1780–1860: a survey', in J. Mokyr, ed., *The economics of the industrial revolution* (London, 1985), pp. 53–74.

McCulloch, J.R., *A statistical account of the British empire*, 2 vols. (London, 1837).

Macfarlane, A., *Witchcraft in Tudor and Stuart England: a regional and comparative study* (London, 1970).

The origins of English individualism: the family, property and social transition (Oxford, 1978).

Malthus, T.R., *An essay on the principle of population* (1798), in E.A. Wrigley and D. Souden, eds., *The works of Thomas Robert Malthus*, 8 vols. (London, 1986), vol. i.

An essay on the principle of population (1826), in Wrigley and Souden, eds., *The works of Thomas Robert Malthus*, vols. ii and iii.

Principles of political economy considered with a view to their practical application, in Wrigley and Souden, eds., *The works of Thomas Robert Malthus*, vols. v and vi.

'On political economy' (review article), in Wrigley and Souden, eds., *The works of Thomas Robert Malthus*, vol. vii, pp. 257–97.

Mathias, P., *The first industrial nation: an economic history of Britain 1700–1914*, 2nd edn (London, 1983).

Medick, H., 'The structures and function of population development under the proto-industrial system', in P. Kriedte, H. Medick and J. Schlumbohn, *Industrialization before industrialization* (Cambridge, 1981), pp. 74–93.

Mendels, F.F., 'Industrialization and population pressure in eighteenth-century Flanders', *J. Econ. Hist.*, xxxi (1971). pp. 269–71.

'Proto-industrialization: the first phase of the industrialization process', *J. Econ. Hist.*, xxxii (1972), pp. 241–61.

Mill, J.S., *Principles of political economy with some of their applications to social philosophy*, ed. J.M. Robson, 2 vols. (Toronto, 1965).

Mitchell, B.R., *Abstract of British historical statistics* (Cambridge, 1962).

European historical statistics 1750–1975, 2nd rev. edn (London, 1981).

Mokyr, J., 'The industrial revolution and the New Economic History', in J. Mokyr, ed., *The economics of the industrial revolution* (London, 1985), pp. 1–51.

Mulhall, M.G., *Dictionary of statistics*, 4th rev. edn (London, 1899).

Musson, A.E., *The growth of British industry* (London, 1978).

Nef, J.U., *The rise of the British coal industry*, 2 vols. (London, 1932).

Newman Brown, W., 'The receipt of poor relief and family situation: Aldenham, Hertfordshire 1630–90', in R.M. Smith, ed., *Land, kinship and life-cycle* (Cambridge, 1984), pp. 405–22.

O'Brien, P., 'Agriculture and the home market for English industry: 1660–1820', *Eng. Hist. Rev.*, c (1985), pp. 773–800.

O'Brien, P. and Keyder, C., *Economic growth in Britain and France 1780–1914: two paths to the twentieth century* (London, 1978).

Ogilvie, S.C., 'Corporation and regulation in rural industry: woollen weaving in Württemberg 1590–1740' (unpub. Ph.D. thesis, Univ. of Cambridge, 1985).

Petty, W., *A treatise of taxes and contributions* (1662), in C.H. Hull, ed., *The economic writings of Sir William Petty*, vol. i (New York, 1963), pp. 1–97.

Phelps Brown, E.H. and Hopkins, S.V., 'Seven centuries of the prices of consumables, compared with builders' wage-rates', *Economica*, new ser., xxiii (1956), pp. 296–314.

Pimentel, D., 'Energy flow in the food system', in D. Pimentel and C.W. Hall, eds., *Food and energy resources* (London, 1984), pp. 1–24.

Porter, G.R., *The progress of the nation in its various social and economical relations*, new edn (London, 1851).

Postan, M.M., 'The historical method in social science', in N.B. Harte, ed., *The study of economic history: collected inaugural lectures 1893–1970* (London, 1971), pp. 127–41.

Pounds, N.J.G., 'Barton farming in eighteenth-century Cornwall', *Journal of the Royal Institution of Cornwall*, new ser., vii (1973), pp. 55–75.

Preston, S.H., Keyfitz, N. and Schoen, R., *Causes of death: life tables for national populations* (New York, 1972).

Ricardo, D., *On the principles of political economy and taxation*, in P. Sraffa, ed., *The works and correspondence of David Ricardo*, vol. i (Cambridge, 1951).

Rostow, W.W., *How it all began: origins of the modern economy* (London, 1975).

Salaman, R.N., *The history and social influence of the potato*, ed. J.G. Hawkes (Cambridge, 1985).

Schofield, R., 'English marriage patterns revisited', *J. Fam. Hist.*, x (1985), pp. 2–20.

Schultz, T.P., *Economics of population* (Reading, Mass., 1981).

Schumpeter, J.A., *History of economic analysis*, ed. E.B. Schumpeter (London, 1954).

Slicher van Bath, B.H., *Een samenleving onder spanning. Geschiedenis van het platteland in Overijssel* (Assen, 1957).

Smith, A., *An inquiry into the nature and causes of the wealth of nations*, new edn, ed. J.R. McCulloch (Edinburgh, 1863).

An inquiry into the nature and causes of the wealth of nations, ed. E. Cannan, 2 vols., orig. pub. 1904 (Chicago, 1976).

Smith, R.M., 'Fertility, economy and household formation in England over three centuries', *Pop. Dev. Rev.*, VII (1981), pp. 595–622.

'Some issues concerning families and their property in rural England 1250–1800', in R.M. Smith, ed., *Land, kinship and life-cycle* (Cambridge, 1984), pp. 1–86.

Stone, R., *Some British empiricists in the social sciences* (the 1986 Mattioli Lectures, forthcoming).

Tann, J., 'Fuel saving in the process industries during the industrial revolution: a study in technological diffusion', *Bus. Hist.*, XV (1973), pp. 149–59.

Tench, W., *A narrative of the expedition to Botany Bay* (1789), in L.F. Fitzhardinge, introd., *Sydney's first four years* (Sydney, 1961), pp. 1–120.

Thirsk, J., *Economic policy and projects: the development of a consumer society in early modern England* (Oxford, 1978).

Thompson, F.M.L., 'Nineteenth-century horse sense', *Econ. Hist. Rev.*, 2nd ser., XXIX (1976), pp. 60–81.

Thomson, D., 'The decline of social welfare: falling state support for the elderly since early Victorian times', *Ageing and Society*, IV (1984), pp. 451–82.

Tönnies, F., *Community and society*, trans. and ed. C.P. Loomis (New York, 1957).

Ubbelohde, A.R., *Man and energy* (London, 1954).

Unger, R.W., 'Energy sources for the Dutch golden age: peat, wind and coal', *Research in Economic History*, IX (1984), pp. 221–53.

United Nations, Department of Economic and Social Affairs, Population Studies, no. 50, *The determinants and consequences of population trends: new summary*, 2 vols. (New York, 1973).

Veblen, T., *Imperial Germany and the industrial revolution*, new edn (London, 1939).

Viazzo, P., *Upland communities: environment, population and social structure in the Alps* (Cambridge, forthcoming).

Ville, S., 'Total factor productivity in the English shipping industry: the north-east coal trade, 1700–1850', *Econ. Hist. Rev.*, 2nd ser., XXXIX (1986), pp. 355–70.

von Thünen, J.H., *The isolated state*, English edn of *Der isolirte Staat in Beziehung auf Landwirtschaft und Nationalökonomie*, ed. P. Hall (Oxford, 1966).

von Tunzelmann, G.N., *Steam power and British industrialization to 1860* (Oxford, 1978).

'Trends in real wages, 1750–1850, revisited', *Econ. Hist. Rev.*, 2nd ser., xxxii (1979), p. 33–49.

Wales, T., 'Poverty, poor relief and the life-cycle: some evidence from seventeenth-century Norfolk', in R.M. Smith, ed., *Land, kinship and life-cycle* (Cambridge, 1986), pp. 351–404.

Weir, D.R., 'Rather never than late: celibacy and age at marriage in English cohort fertility', *J. Fam. Hist.*, ix (1984), pp. 340–54.

White, L.P. and Plaskett, L.G., *Biomass as fuel* (London, 1981).

Woods, R., 'The effects of population redistribution on the level of mortality in nineteenth-century England and Wales', *J. Econ. Hist.*, xlv (1985), pp. 645–51.

Wrigley, E.A., 'The supply of raw materials in the industrial revolution', *Econ. Hist. Rev.*, 2nd ser., xv (1962), pp. 1–16.

Population and history (London, 1969).

'The process of modernization and the industrial revolution in England', *Journal of Interdisciplinary History*, iii (1972), pp. 225–59.

'Marriage, fertility and population growth in eighteenth-century England', in R.B. Outhwaite, ed., *Marriage and society: studies in the social history of marriage* (London, 1981), pp. 137–85.

'The growth of population in eighteenth-century England: a conundrum resolved', *P. & P.*, xcviii (1983), pp. 121–50.

'Men on the land and men in the countryside: employment in agriculture in early nineteenth-century England', in L. Bonfield, R.M. Smith and K. Wrightson, eds., *The world we have gained: histories of population and social structure* (Oxford, 1986), pp. 295–336.

'Urban growth and agricultural change: England and the continent in the early modern period', in R.I. Rotberg and T.K. Rabb, eds., *Population and economy: population and history from the traditional to the modern world* (Cambridge, 1986), pp. 123–86.

'The classical economists and the industrial revolution', in E.A. Wrigley, *People, cities and wealth: the transformation of traditional society* (Oxford, 1987), pp. 21–45.

'Some reflections on corn yields and prices in pre-industrial economies', in Wrigley, *People, cities and wealth*, pp. 92–130.

'The fall of marital fertility in nineteenth-century France', in Wrigley, *People, cities and wealth*, pp. 270–321.

'The limits to growth: Malthus and the classical economists', in M. Teitelbaum, ed., *Population, resources and environment: the interplay of science, ideology and intellectual traditions* (forthcoming).

Wrigley, E.A. and Schofield, R.S., *The population history of England 1541–1871: a reconstruction* (London, 1981).

'English population history from family reconstitution: summary results 1600–1799', *Pop. Stud.*, xxxvii (1983), pp. 157–84.

Young, A., *Political arithmetic: containing observations on the present state of Great Britain* (London, 1779).

Travels in France during the years 1787, 1788 and 1789, ed. J. Kaplow (New York, 1969).

Index